The Pilot's
R/T Handbook

The Pilot's R/T Handbook

Christopher Leech

Airlife

First published in 2006 by
Airlife Publishing, an imprint of
The Crowood Press Ltd
Ramsbury, Marlborough
Wiltshire SN8 2HR

www.crowood.com

British Library Cataloguing-in-Publication Data
A catalogue record for this book is available from the British Library.

ISBN 1 86126 853 X
EAN 978 1 86126 853 2

Typeset by SR Nova Pvt Ltd., Bangalore, India

Printed and bound in Great Britain by Biddles Ltd, King's Lynn

CONTENTS

LIST OF ABBREVIATIONS

AAL	Above Aerodrome Level
ADF	Automatic Direction Finder
AGL	Above Ground Level
AIP	Aeronautical Information Publication
ANO	Air Navigation Order
ATC	Air Traffic Control
ATCO	Air Traffic Control Officer
ATCU	Air Traffic Control Unit
ATIS	Automatic Terminal Information Service
ATPL	Airline Transport Pilots Licence
ATSOCAs	Air Traffic Services Outside Controlled Airspace
ATSU	Air Traffic Service Unit
ATZ	Aerodrome Traffic Zone
CAA	Civil Aviation Authority
CAP	Civil Aviation Publication
CPL	Commercial Pilot's Licence
D&D	Distress and Diversion
DAAIS	Danger Area Activity Information Service
DACS	Danger Area Crossing Service
DF	Direction Finding
DI	Direction Indicator
DME	Distance Measuring Equipment
DR	Dead Reckoning
EAT	Estimated Arrival Time
ETA	Estimated Time of Arrival
FIR	Flight Information Region
FIS	Flight Information Service
FISO	Flight Information Service Officer
FL	Flight Level
FMS	Flight Management System
FRTOL	Flight Radiotelephony Operator's Licence
ft	feet (measurement)
GA	General Aviation
GPS	Global Positioning System
HF	High Frequency
Hz	Hertz (unit of frequency)
IFR	Instrument Flight Rules
ILS	Instrument Landing System
IMC	Instrument Meteorological Conditions
JAA	Joint Aviation Authority
JAR	Joint Aviation Requirements
JAR-FCL	JAR-Flight Crew Licensing
kHz	kilohertz
kt	knots (nautical miles per hour)
LARS	Lower Airspace Radar Service
LVPs	Low Visibility Procedures
MATZ	Military Aerodrome Traffic Zone
Mb	Millibars
MHz	megahertz
NDB	Non-Directional Beacon
NPPL	National Private Pilots Licence
PIC	Pilot In Command
POB	People On Board
PPL	Private Pilots Licence
PTT	Press To Talk (button)
RAS	Radar Advisory Service
RIS	Radar Information Service
R/T	Radiotelephony
SID	Standard Instrument Departure
SSR	Secondary Surveillance Radar
StAr	Standard Arrival
SVFR	Special Visual Flight Rules
TCAS	Traffic alert & Collision Avoidance System
UTC	Universal Time Coordinated
VDF	VHF Direction Finding
VFR	Visual Flight Rules
VHF	Very High Frequency
VMC	Visual Meteorological Conditions
VOR	VHF Omni Range (beacon)

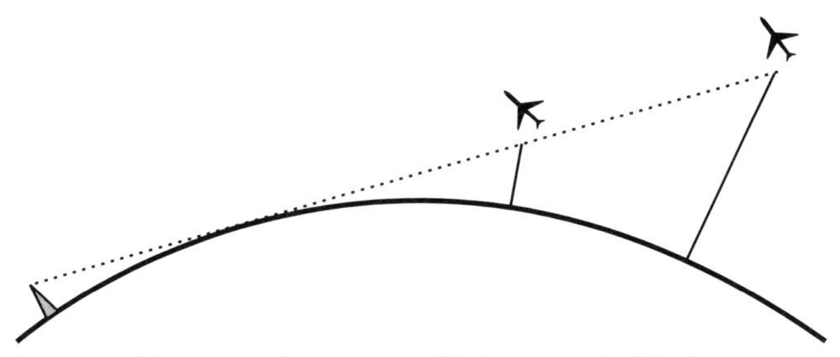

Increased transmission range with increased altitude.

Radio waves in this part of the spectrum are considered to travel in straight lines – this is not strictly true, but is good enough for our purposes. Therefore, communication is 'line of sight' only; in other words, the furthest point you can see is the furthest point you can communicate with. This makes VHF limited by the curvature of the earth and therefore only suitable for short-range communication, but an advantage of this lack of 'over-the-horizon' transmission is that more than one ground station can use the same frequency without interference, provided that they are sufficiently far apart.

Another important implication of this characteristic is that the higher the transmitter and/or receiver, the greater the possible range – a fact worth remembering when lost and unable to receive the station you were communicating with.

A final advantage of the VHF band is that it is relatively unaffected by atmospheric and weather conditions, though strong electromagnetic phenomena such as auroras and highly charged storm cells may cause some interference.

Frequencies within the aviation VHF band are published as megahertz and decimals thereof. In lower airspace the frequencies are allocated at intervals of 25kHz (0.025MHz), and so starting with the lowest aviation frequency, as you turn the frequency selector on the radio, the steps run:

118.000
118.025
118.050
118.075
118.100
118.125

and so on up to 136.975

In R/T phraseology, radio frequencies are always transmitted by articulating all six digits separately, and using the word 'DECIMAL' at the appropriate place:

118.025 ONE ONE EIGHT DECIMAL ZERO TWO FIVE

118.050 ONE ONE EIGHT DECIMAL ZERO FIVE ZERO

The only exception to this is when the final two digits are both zero, in which case only the first four digits need be transmitted:

118.100 ONE ONE EIGHT DECIMAL ONE

With increasing congestion in the aviation VHF band it has become necessary to make more frequencies available by further subdividing the spectrum into 8.33kHz subdivisions. This effectively squeezes two more frequencies into each of the 25kHz steps mentioned above. As yet this narrow spacing is only used in upper airspace, and most light aircraft do not have radios equipped to tune these 8.33-spaced frequencies.

Radio sets able to transmit and receive 8.33-spaced frequencies tend to be found in commercial and airways-equipped aircraft, and these are referred to as being 'eight point three three capable'. Since it is mandatory to be 8.33-capable to operate in some volumes of airspace, the controller may enquire if an aircraft is so equipped:

BRITISH ONE TWO ALPHA, ARE YOU EIGHT POINT THREE THREE EQUIPPED

> AFFIRM EIGHT POINT THREE THREE, BRITISH ONE TWO ALPHA
>
> or
>
> NEGATIVE EIGHT POINT THREE THREE, BRITISH ONE TWO ALPHA.

HF Transmissions

The High Frequency band runs from 3 to 30MHz. Radio waves in this part of the spectrum are refracted back to earth in the ionosphere as a 'skywave', thus making 'over-the-horizon' communication possible. These properties make HF suitable for long-range communication, though they also make HF transmissions more susceptible to interference from atmospheric and weather conditions.

The main use of HF radiotelephony is in commercial operations, so HF radios are mainly to be found in commercial aircraft. However, the general phraseology is the same as that used for VHF.

AIRCRAFT RADIO EQUIPMENT

An airborne radio consists of three basic parts: the transceiver (transmitter and receiver), a control unit and the antennae. Where more than one radio is fitted an audio selector box or station box is needed to allow the pilot(s) to select between radios, and an intercom allows the aircraft crew to communicate with each other. Finally, all of these need to be connected to the microphones and speakers of either headphones or cabin speakers and hand microphones.

The layout and controls of aircraft radios vary with age, manufacturer and the sophistication of the radio specification, so it is impossible to provide a detailed description of every possible fit. However, while the presentation may vary, there are a number of controls that are common to most of the radio fits that the average pilot is likely to encounter.

Radios

In a light aircraft the radio(s) are usually situated in the instrument panel, the transceiver and its controls being integrated as a single unit. The controls are typically as follows:

On/off switch: apart from the 'off' and 'on' positions there will usually be a 'test' position that creates a static noise as a test signal.

Volume: (may be combined with the on/off switch) controls the volume of reception only – not the transmitted volume. Where more than radio is fitted each radio will have its own volume control.

Frequency selector: this is often a dual rotary knob, the outer dial controlling the megahertz (numbers before the decimal point), the inner controlling the kilohertz (numbers after the decimal point). Modern sets may have two frequencies displayed, one 'active' and the other 'standby'. The frequency controller changes the standby frequency, which can then be shunted over to the active position by the 'flip flop' button. Apart from being able to preset a frequency and have it waiting for use when needed, the great advantage of this system is that the previous active frequency is shunted back to the standby window when the new frequency is activated, so if you have misdialled the new frequency the old one is still there to go back to. Older sets may change frequency in steps of 0.050MHz, and have a separate method of selecting frequencies at 0.025MHz spacing. This is usually done either with a separate switch or by pulling the normal frequency selector knob out.

Squelch: when there are no transmissions on a frequency, the receiver will pick up background static. To prevent this unwanted noise being heard in the headphones or on speaker, the squelch suppresses the output from the receiver. However, if the level of suppression is set too high, weak transmissions could also be lost: if the squelch is adjustable, the usual technique is to turn the rotary knob until the background hiss just disappears. Newer sets may have an automatic squelch with a simple on/off push button.

Push To Talk (PTT) button: with the radio on and set correctly reception is passive – that is, you will hear anything said on the frequency in use – but to transmit, the pilot must press the PTT button, which is usually

Typical modern light aircraft radios.

located on the instrument panel or the control yoke. There is usually also a transmission indicator that illuminates when that radio is actually transmitting; this may be a simple light or, in an electronic display, a 'Tx' caption. This provides both a check that the equipment is transmitting and, perhaps more importantly, that it has stopped transmitting when you think it has, which may not always be the case if you have a stuck PTT button.

Audio Selector Box

This allows the pilot to configure the output from and input to the radios, selecting which radio to use, and between use of headphones or speakers for reception. Its controls are typically as follows:

Transmitter selector: selects the radio box that transmissions will be made on.

Audio selectors: selects which radio boxes are audible, and switches reception between either the headphones or the cabin speakers.

Auto audio selector: couples audio reception to the transmitter selection, so that audio is automatically received on the box that is selected for transmission.

While it is only possible to select one box to transmit at any one time, the controls described above allow the pilot to listen out on more than one radio simultaneously. Apart from providing redundancy in the event of any one radio failing, this sort of multiple radio fit also allows collection of weather data, from ATIS or Volmet, on the second radio while maintaining communication with ATC on the main set. Having said that, the pilot's primary duty is to monitor the ATC frequency in use, and weather data collection should only be attempted when safe operation permits. It is entirely reasonable when operating 'single pilot' to request Air Traffic to pass any weather or other information required when cockpit workload is high.

Intercom

This allows the pilot(s) to communicate with each other and with other people in the aircraft. Speech on the intercom is not transmitted outside the aircraft unless the PTT button is pressed. Its controls are typically as follows:

On/off switch: turns the intercom on or off.

Volume: sets intercom volume independently of the radios.

Isolator: there may be the facility to isolate part of the intercom system, such as the rear seats, to prevent unwanted noise (and 'back-seat drivers'!).

The use of headsets is now more or less universal. These consist of a speaker held over each of the pilot's ears by a headband, and a microphone on a flexible boom that allows it to be positioned in front of the mouth. Ear seals provide a comfortable fit and reduce external noise, and most headsets now have a built-in volume control (some have a separate control for each ear) in the form of a rotary knob on the speaker housing. The headset is connected to the aircraft radio system by inserting jack plugs into the appropriate sockets.

Typical modern light aircraft communication and navigation suite.

A two-plug system is the most common (one for the microphone and the other for the speakers), each plug and socket being of a slightly different size from the other plug and socket so that it is fairly safe to assume that if you've got both in, they're the right way round.

While the use of hand microphones and cabin speakers has largely died out in light aircraft, these may still be fitted as a backup. The PTT switch for a hand mic is usually incorporated in the hand mic housing itself. The great disadvantage of a hand mic is that its use requires the pilot to remove one hand from the controls.

In larger commercial aircraft the radios are usually situated in an avionics rack, with control units in the pilots' instrument panels. Each pilot has their own station box giving each independent access to all the aircraft's communication systems. Apart from providing redundancy, such a system allows one pilot to remain on the ATC frequency in use, while the other is able to gather weather data and communicate with company operations on the other radio. With the increasing use of Electronic Flight Information Systems, the displays of the communication systems, navaids, transponders and traffic-avoidance systems may be combined and presented to the pilots on a cathode ray tube based unit called a Radio Management Unit.

Station box.

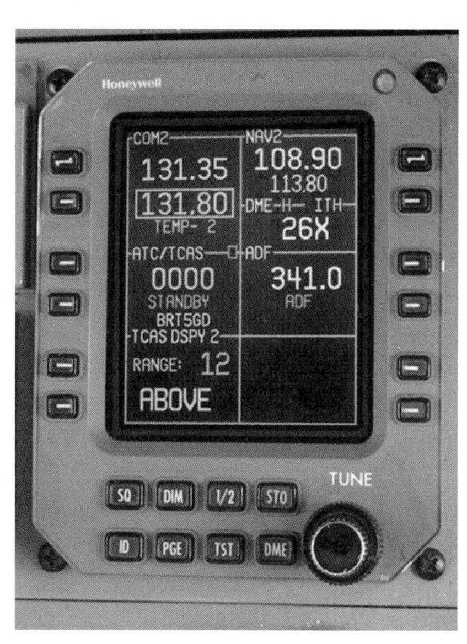

Radio Management Unit.

Chapter 2 Regulation and the Structure of Air Traffic Services

LICENSING AND CERTIFICATION

Flight Radiotelephony Operator's Licence

A pilot's licence by itself does not confer the right to operate aircraft radio equipment. No person may operate an aircraft station in the air or on the ground unless they are in possession of a Flight Radiotelephony Operator's Licence (FRTOL), or are operating directly under the supervision of a FRTOL holder.

A FRTOL is not a prerequisite for the issue of a pilot's licence, and it is in theory possible to gain a pilot's licence and operate without a FRTOL, though this would restrict the pilot to operation outside controlled airspace which, given the crowded ATC environment in the United Kingdom, would be quite limiting.

While the FRTOL may be issued as a standalone licence, it is usually issued in conjunction with a pilot's licence, the necessary training being conducted during the PPL course. In order to allow a student pilot to undertake solo flights, the regulations exempt aircrew under training from the need to hold a FRTOL to operate the aircraft radios, provided that they are operating under the direction of a flying instructor. Communication training forms a mandatory part of the JAR-FCL PPL training course, and is recommended for the UK NPPL. Applicants for the JAR-FCL PPL must pass the communications written exam before taking the PPL skills test. The syllabus of practical training is set out in Appendix V.

To be able to apply for the FRTOL, the student is required to pass a multi-choice theoretical examination and a Practical Communications Test. The Practical Communications Test takes the form of a simulated flight, conducted in the classroom, in which the candidate acts as the pilot while the examiner, connected to the candidate via an Approved Radio Simulator, plays the part of various Air Traffic Service Units. The route from one airfield to another will pass through a Military Aerodrome Traffic Zone and include an emergency, as well as other possible scenarios such as a control zone crossing. The candidate is supplied with a route map, a navigation plan and a list of communication facilities, and is required to make all the appropriate radio calls and frequency selections as though he was actually flying the route.

The FRTOL allows the holder to operate the radios in any aircraft, but not aeronautical ground stations. The privileges are limited to VHF only: it does not include the use of HF unless the holder has either passed an additional HF radio theory examination, or holds a UK or JAA professional pilot's licence (CPL or ATPL).

When issued in conjunction with a pilot's licence the FRTOL is valid for the same period as the pilot's licence to which it is attached, and there is no separate fee for issue (one of the very few times you ever get anything for nothing in aviation!). The FRTOL is automatically reissued when the pilot's licence is renewed.

Aircraft Radio Licence

An aircraft radio station (that is, a radio in an aircraft), whether installed or portable, requires an Aircraft Radio Licence, which must be renewed annually. It is the responsibility of a FRTOL holder to ensure that the radio station he is operating has a valid licence. In addition, the installation itself requires a Certificate of Approval for Radio Installation, which must be reapplied for if any significant changes are made.

CLASSIFICATION OF AIRSPACE

Class A: Terminal Manoeuvring Areas/Zones, Control Areas and Airways. IFR flights only permitted. All flights are subject to ATC service and are separated from each other.

Class B: In the UK this only exists above Flight Level 245. IFR and VFR flights permitted. All flights are subject to ATC service and are separated from each other.

Class C: Not currently allocated in UK airspace. IFR and VFR flights permitted. All flights are subject to ATC service. IFR flights are separated from each other and from VFR flights.

Class D: Control Areas/Zones around significant commercial airfields. IFR and VFR flights permitted. All flights are subject to ATC service. IFR flights are separated from each other, and receive traffic information relating to VFR flights.

Class E: IFR and VFR flights permitted. All flights subject to ATC service. IFR flights are separated from each other. All flights receive traffic information if practicable.

All flights in airspace classified A to E are subject to ATC service, and therefore these classifications are categorized as Controlled Airspace.

Class F: Advisory Airspace/Routes. IFR and VFR flights permitted. All participating IFR flights receive an air traffic advisory service. All flights receive a Flight Information Service if requested.

Class G: The open Flight Information Region (FIR). IFR and VFR flights permitted. All flights receive Flight Information Service if requested.

Flights in airspace classified F and G may operate without an ATC service, and therefore these classifications are categorised as Uncontrolled Airspace.

Aerodrome Traffic Zones (ATZ) take their classification from the airspace in which the airfield is situated, and the rules that apply will be those appropriate to the type of ATSU operating at that airfield, as discussed below.

THE STRUCTURE AND AUTHORITY OF AERONAUTICAL COMMUNICATION SERVICES

While we commonly use the phrase 'air traffic control' to refer to all classes of air/ground communication, this is in fact incorrect, as the title Air Traffic Control refers specifically to one of the classifications of aeronautical communication services. There are three of these classifications, which are as follows:

Air Traffic Control Service (ATC): Provided by a licensed Air Traffic Control Officer (ATCO) in circumstances regulated by the CAA.

Flight Information Service (FIS): Provided by a licensed Flight Information Service Officer (FISO) in circumstances regulated by the CAA.

Air/Ground Communication Service (at an aerodrome): Provided by a Radio Operator who holds a Certificate of Competency, and operates under the jurisdiction of the holder of the radio installation licence.

Each of the Aeronautical Communication Services mentioned above carries a different level of responsibility and authority, and the pilot needs to understand the practical implications of each of these in order to be able to use the service correctly.

Air Traffic Control Service

An Air Traffic Control Officer is able to issue instructions and to grant or withhold permissions within the airspace he controls. Examples of this may be permission to enter the airspace he controls or permission to land or take off. Put simply, he can tell you what to do and what not to do. This doesn't mean that you are no longer the aircraft commander or responsible for the safe conduct of the flight; however, if you are not going to comply with Air Traffic Control instructions you need a very good reason for not doing so, and you must inform the Air Traffic Control Officer of this using the phrase 'UNABLE COMPLY', usually followed by a brief explanation of why.

Flight Information Service

A Flight Information Service Officer provides information, and it is then up to pilot to use that information to decide on the best course of action. Flight Information Services are available at some airfields (an Aerodrome Flight Information Service) and in the open FIRs.

An Aerodrome Flight Information Service provides information about conditions at the aerodrome and within the Aerodrome Traffic Zone. At an aerodrome a FISO may issue instructions to aircraft moving on the apron and other specified parts of the ground manoeuvring area, but he may not issue instructions to aircraft elsewhere on the ground or anywhere in the air, though he may request position reports. In other words, when it comes to entering a runway, taking off, landing or performing any in-flight manoeuvre it is solely your responsibility to make sure it is safe to do so.

Flight Information Service is available in the open FIR twenty-four hours a day, but there is no requirement to establish contact with the service. The service is entirely procedural (i.e. with no radar), so the FISO will only be aware of those flights that do make contact.

A Flight Information Service Officer may relay clearances from an Air Traffic Control Unit (ATCU) provided he makes it clear from which ATCU the instruction originates.

Air/Ground Communication Service

The Radio Operator can provide any useful aerodrome information to a pilot that he is aware of. There is no requirement for the Radio Operator to be able to see any of the aerodrome, so all the information may be based on the reports of other pilots. A Radio Operator may not issue any instructions, so basically everything is up to the pilot.

A Radio Operator may relay clearances from an Air Traffic Control Unit provided he makes it clear from which ATCU the instruction originates.

CALLSIGNS OF AERONAUTICAL GROUND STATIONS

By now you have probably worked out that Air Traffic Control happens at larger airfields that probably have commercial traffic, while FIS and A/G radio are likely to be found at smaller airfields generally dealing with light and general aviation. If you are unsure what type of service you are receiving, you can determine this from the callsign of the station.

The callsign of an aeronautical ground station is made up of two elements: a geographical location (or, if offshore, the name of the vessel or structure) and a suffix indicating the type of service provided.

Air Traffic Control Service

Location: either the name of the airfield (e.g. HEATHROW) or the name of the control centre for the volume of airspace under the control of the ATCU (e.g. LONDON).

Suffix: this will depend on the type of service provided, as follows:

CONTROL:	Area control
RADAR:	General radar
APPROACH:	Approach control
DIRECTOR:	Approach control radar
DEPARTURE:	Departure control radar
TOWER:	Aerodrome control
GROUND:	Ground movement control
DELIVERY:	Ground movement planning and clearance delivery
TALKDOWN:	Precision approach radar control (mainly military).

Flight Information Service

Location: either the name of the airfield (e.g. KEMBLE) or the name of the FIR (either LONDON or SCOTTISH) for which the information service is available.
Suffix: INFORMATION.

Air/Ground Communication Service

Location: the name of the airfield (e.g. DUNKESWELL).
Suffix: RADIO.

On initial contact the full callsign of the station should be used (e.g. 'HEATHROW TOWER'), but once communication is established, and provided there is no possibility of confusion, you may then abbreviate the callsign to either just the location or suffix (e.g. 'HEATHROW' or 'TOWER').

From the above list we can see that Flight Information Services and Air/Ground Communication Services only have one callsign suffix ('INFORMATION' and 'RADIO', respectively), while an Air Traffic Control Service may have a number of callsign suffixes depending on the service provided. However, just because an airfield provides Air Traffic Control, it does not mean that it has all the controllers listed. An airfield just busy enough to warrant a single ATC frequency will have a 'Tower' controller who has to do all the approach and ground control as well. As airfields get bigger, further controllers are added, and the job of the tower controller shrinks down to controlling just the runway and its immediate approaches (including the visual circuit).

The level of service may be different at different times as well: for example, a ground frequency could operate at busy times of day, but at quieter times the frequency may be closed and ground control taken over by the tower. Alternatively, a smaller airfield may offer an Aerodrome Flight Information Service if busy at weekends, but downgrade to an Air/Ground Communication Service midweek.

RECORDED INFORMATION BROADCASTS

For larger airfields, in order to prevent frequencies becoming clogged up with pilots requesting and receiving weather data, there may be a recorded information broadcast. These are voice recordings of weather data and other important aerodrome information and they come in two formats:

Automatic Terminal Information Service (ATIS): provides data for a single airfield. Broadcast range is relatively short.

Volmet: provides data for a number of airfields. Broadcast range is relatively long, and primarily intended for inbound commercial traffic.

The information is continuously repeated, so if you miss something it will come round again if you wait. The information is usually updated every half

Surveillance radar head with a secondary surveillance radar head on top.

Ground movement radar head.

Summary of Aeronautical Communication Services

Service	Callsign	Personnel	Authority
Air Traffic Control	CONTROL RADAR APPROACH DIRECTOR DEPARTURE TOWER GROUND DELIVERY TALKDOWN	Licensed Air Traffic Control Officer	Issue instructions, grant or withhold permissions.
Flight Information	INFORMATION	Licensed Flight Information Service Officer	Provide information. Issue instructions to aircraft moving on the apron and other specified parts of the ground manoeuvring area only.
Air/Ground Communication	RADIO	Radio Operator who holds a Certificate of Competency	Provide information.
Recorded Information	ATIS VOLMET		

hour, although if a particularly significant change occurs it should be updated sooner. Very large airfields may have one ATIS for arriving aircraft and a separate ATIS for departing aircraft.

Volmets are rather like several ATIS broadcasts from different airfields joined together, although the exact content varies slightly. The format of ATIS and Volmet messages, along with specific words and phrases associated with them, are detailed in Appendix III.

FREQUENCIES AND OTHER INFORMATION

To establish contact with an aeronautical communication service, you need to know its frequency. The definitive source of this information is the UK Air Information Publication (UK AIP), an up-to-date copy of which should be available, along with Notams detailing any recent changes, at any reasonable briefing facility. Apart from information on the frequencies themselves, other details provided include callsigns, hours of watch and other useful information.

Some frequencies are also printed on the 1:5,000,000 charts, and there are also a number of commercially available flight guides; the latter are usually tailored to a particular sort of operation, such as IFR or VFR, and therefore vary in the extent of information included.

Most commercial flight guides offer an amendment service (for a price), but with all of these it is worth remembering, that because the information changes from time to time, it will only be valid as of the last publication or amendment date.

As mentioned in the previous chapter, the range of VHF communication is limited by the curvature of the earth's surface, so different ground stations can use the same frequency without interference provided they are sufficiently far apart. This spacing of the allocation of frequencies is carefully planned to provide protection from interference between two stations using the same frequency. At major airports the frequencies are protected as follows:

- Tower: 25 miles and 4,000ft height;
- Approach: 25 miles and 10,000ft height.

To prevent interference the CAA recommends that, at smaller airfields, communication is *ideally* limited to the immediate vicinity of the airfield and not above a height of 1,000ft. The latter stipulation is a bit unrealistic, so they also say that in any event it should be restricted to not more than 10 miles, and not above a height of 3,000ft from the field.

PRIORITY OF MESSAGES

A little thought will make you realize that some transmissions are more important than others. For example, emergency messages take precedence over all other communications. To help controllers and pilots deal with the differing importance of communications, messages are categorized and, where frequency congestion exists, handled in the following priority order:

1. distress messages (*see* Chapter 7);
2. urgency messages (*see* Chapter 7);
3. messages relating to direction finding;
4. flight safety messages; general air traffic control;
5. meteorological messages;
6. flight regularity messages – mainly aircraft operating agency/company messages.

CHAPTER 3 THE BASIC BUILDING BLOCKS OF RADIOTELEPHONY

In order to get started we now need to understand the basic building blocks of practical aviation radiotelephony, which are:

- transmitting technique;
- the phonetic alphabet, and numerology;
- standard words and phrases;
- conventions;
- callsigns and their abbreviations;
- read-back requirements; and
- general message structure.

Each of these will now be discussed in turn.

TRANSMITTING TECHNIQUE

Do:

- check equipment set-up – correct frequency selected and volume set;
- listen out before transmitting – do not transmit over an existing conversation;
- know what you intend to say;
- fully depress the PTT switch before starting to speak, and keep it fully depressed until you are finished;
- speak clearly, and maintain an even volume and rate of speech (not more than 100 words per minute);
- use standard words and phraseology;
- keep it short; and
- be ready to copy down any reply.

Do not:

- use excessive courtesies, unnecessary words and fillers such as 'um' and 'er';
- turn your head away from a hand microphone;
- hold the boom of a headset microphone; or
- have the microphone touching your lips.

THE PHONETIC ALPHABET AND NUMEROLOGY

Letters

To transmit individual letters we use the phonetic alphabet, which is intended to prevent confusion between similar-sounding letters (such as 'M' and 'N') by replacing them with dissimilar-sounding words (MIKE and NOVEMBER), as follows:

Letter	Word	Letter	Word
A	ALPHA	N	NOVEMBER
B	BRAVO	O	OSCAR
C	CHARLIE	P	PAPA
D	DELTA	Q	QUEBEC
E	ECHO	R	ROMEO
F	FOXTROT	S	SIERRA
G	GOLF	T	TANGO
H	HOTEL	U	UNIFORM
I	INDIA	V	VICTOR
J	JULIET	W	WHISKEY
K	KILO	X	X-RAY
L	LIMA	Y	YANKEE
M	MIKE	Z	ZULU

Numbers

Individual numbers are transmitted as follows:

Number	Pronunciation	Number	Pronunciation
0	ZERO	5	FIFE
1	WUN	6	SIX
2	TOO	7	SEVEN
3	TREE	8	AIT
4	FOWER	9	NINER
Hundred	HUNDRED	Thousand	TOUSAND

Generally, multi-digit numbers are transmitted by speaking each digit separately:

heading 100 — HEADING WUN ZERO ZERO.

A decimal point is indicated by the word decimal, pronounced 'DAY-SEE-MAL', at the appropriate position:

frequency 133.850 — FREQUENCY WUN TREE TREE DAYSEEMAL AIT FIFE ZERO.

The words 'HUNDRED' or 'THOUSAND' are to be used in numbers relating to vertical measurements (height, altitude, flight level, cloud height) and visibility (including runway visual ranges), that contain whole hundreds or thousands. Each digit of the number of hundreds or thousands is said separately followed by the word 'HUNDRED' or 'THOUSAND' as appropriate:

altitude 2,000ft — ALTITUDE TOO TOUSAND FEET.

altitude 22,000ft — ALTITUDE TOO TOO TOUSAND FEET.

flight level 100 — FLIGHT LEVEL WUN HUNDRED.

But note that flight level 110, since it is not a whole hundred would be said:

FLIGHT LEVEL WUN WUN ZERO.

If the number consists of thousands and whole hundreds, the number of thousands is said followed by 'THOUSAND', then the number of hundreds followed by 'HUNDRED':

altitude 2,500ft — ALTITUDE TOO TOUSAND FIFE HUNDRED FEET.

altitude 22,500ft — ALTITUDE TOO TOO TOUSAND FIFE HUNDRED FEET.

Summary of When to Use/Not to Use 'HUNDRED' or 'THOUSAND'

'HUNDRED' or 'THOUSAND' used when number contains whole hundreds or thousands	**Each digit to be articulated separately**
height	Everything else including:
altitude	headings
flight level	altimeter and pressure settings
cloud height	frequencies and transponder codes
visibility	wind speed and direction
runway	
visual range	

For brevity, and in order to highlight the difference in the phraseology examples given in later chapters, numerals will be used when each digit is to be spoken separately (e.g. 100 spoken WUN ZERO ZERO), but will be written out in words when HUNDREDs or THOUSANDs can be used. (e.g. 100 spoken WUN HUNDRED). We will also go back to normal spelling, but the pronunciation described above is to be used.

STANDARD WORDS AND PHRASES

ACKNOWLEDGE — Acknowledge that you have received and understood the message (an instruction, not a reply).

GOLF CHARLIE DELTA, STOP CLIMB TWO THOUSAND FEET, ACKNOWLEDGE.

AFFIRM — Yes.

APPROVED — The proposed course of action is approved.

TOWER, WESSEX 10, REQUEST LEFT 20 DEGREES DUE WEATHER.

WESSEX 10, APPROVED.

BREAK — Indicates a separation between messages to different aircraft.

WESSEX 10, STOP CLIMB TWO THOUSAND FEET, BREAK, BRITISH 12 ALPHA CLEARED IMMEDIATE TAKE OFF.

CANCEL — Cancel the previous clearance.

BRITISH 12 ALPHA, CANCEL LINE UP, REPORT WHEN READY FOR DEPARTURE.

CHANGING TO — I intend to change frequency to a different station/frequency.

CHANGING TO HENFIELD 123.425, GOLF CHARLIE DELTA.

CHECK — Check ... (an instruction, not a reply).

WESSEX 10, CHECK GEAR DOWN.

CLEARED	Authorized to proceed to …
	GOLF CHARLIE DELTA, CLEARED FOR A STANDARD VFR CASTLEHEAD DEPARTURE.
CLIMB	Climb to … (height/altitude/flight level) … and maintain.
	BRITISH 12 ALPHA, CLIMB FLIGHT LEVEL ONE HUNDRED.
CONFIRM	Request you verify …
	CONFIRM RIGHT HAND CIRCUIT, GOLF CHARLIE DELTA.
CONTACT	Establish radio contact with … (station/frequency); your details have been passed to them (*see* FREECALL).
	WESSEX 10, CONTACT WINTERBOURNE APPROACH 126.350.
CORRECT	True (confirmation that something is true, not an instruction).
	GOLF CHARLIE DELTA, CONFIRM YOU INTEND TO LAND OFF THIS APPROACH.
	CORRECT, GOLF CHARLIE DELTA.
CORRECTION	The following is a correction of a previous error.
	BRITISH 12 ALPHA, DESCEND FLIGHT LEVEL ONE HUNDRED, CORRECTION DESCEND FLIGHT LEVEL 110.
DESCEND	Descend to … (height/altitude/flight level) … and maintain.
DISREGARD	Ignore.
EXPEDITE	Perform … as quickly as possible consistent with safety.
	WESSEX 10, EXPEDITE VACATING RUNWAY.

FANSTOP	Practice engine failure (single-engine aircraft). GOLF CHARLIE DELTA, REQUESTS FANSTOP NEXT CIRCUIT.
FREECALL	Establish radio contact with … (station/frequency); your details have not been passed to them (*see* CONTACT). GOLF CHARLIE DELTA, FREECALL HAWKSBURY RADAR 124.150.
HOLD SHORT	Stop before … BRITISH 12 ALPHA, TAXI VIA BRAVO, HOLD SHORT OF THE INTERSECTION WITH CHARLIE.
HOW DO YOU READ	How well do you read my transmissions.
I SAY AGAIN	I will repeat for emphasis or clarity. GOLF CHARLIE DELTA, DANGER AREA 119 IS ACTIVE, I SAY AGAIN, DANGER AREA 119 IS ACTIVE.
MAINTAIN	Continue … (specific parameter). BRITISH 12 ALPHA, MAINTAIN FLIGHT LEVEL 230.
MONITOR	Listen out on … (station/frequency). BRITISH 12 ALPHA, MONITOR TOWER 119.25.
NEGATIVE	No.
PASS YOUR MESSAGE	Transmit your message.
READ BACK	Repeat message exactly as received (may be all or part). WESSEX 10, MAKE YOUR HEADING 150 DEGREES, ON REACHING FLIGHT LEVEL 40, LEFT TURN APPROVED BACK TO THE HOLD, READ BACK CLEARANCE.

HEADING 150 DEGREES, ON REACHING FLIGHT LEVEL 40, LEFT TURN APPROVED BACK TO THE HOLD, WESSEX 10.

REPORT — Provide requested information.

GOLF CHARLIE DELTA, REPORT YOUR ALTITUDE.

REQUEST — I would like to get permission for (a specific manoeuvre), or to obtain (a piece of information).

GOLF CHARLIE DELTA, REQUEST TAXI.

GOLF CHARLIE DELTA, REQUEST THE LATEST WEATHER.

ROGER — Message received and understood.

BRITISH 12 ALPHA, PREVIOUS AIRCRAFT REPORTED WINDSHEAR ON SHORT FINAL.

ROGER, BRITISH 12 ALPHA.

SAY AGAIN — Request to repeat transmission (may be all or part).

SPEAK SLOWER — Reduce rate of transmission.

SQUAWK — Set transponder code.

WESSEX 10, SQUAWK 4172.

STANDBY — Wait until I call you.

FRAMPTON APPROACH, GOLF ALPHA BRAVO CHARLIE DELTA AT CASTLEHEAD, REQUEST JOINING INSTRUCTIONS.

GOLF CHARLIE DELTA, STANDBY.

UNABLE — Unable to comply with instruction (usually followed by explanation).

BRITISH 12 ALPHA, RIGHT TURN HEADING 020.

UNABLE DUE WEATHER, BRITISH 12 ALPHA.

WILCO ('Will comply') I understand your message and will do as requested.

GOLF CHARLIE DELTA, REPORT WHEN YOU HAVE THE FIELD IN SIGHT.

WILCO, GOLF CHARLIE DELTA.

CONVENTIONS

A number of conventions are used to help prevent ambiguity when transmitting levels, headings, pressure settings and time.

Levels

Terms relating to vertical distance have quite specific meanings in aviation:

Term	Meaning	Altimeter Setting
Height	Vertical distance above a specific surface point (usually an airfield reference point or runway threshold)	QFE
Altitude	Vertical distance above mean sea level	QNH
Flight level	The altimeter reading with 1013 set on the subscale, expressed to the nearest 100ft; i.e. with the last two digits omitted. e.g. 7,000ft = FL 70 10,000ft = FL 100	1013Mb (The Standard Setting)

The word 'level' (as opposed to 'flight level') is often used as blanket term to cover all the vertical measurements above.

All reports, instructions and replies relating to a level should include the word(s) 'HEIGHT', 'ALTITUDE' or 'FLIGHT LEVEL', as appropriate.

In order to promote differentiation between altitudes or heights and flight levels, the word 'TO' is always used when giving or reading back altitude or height instructions:

BRITISH 12 ALPHA, CLIMB **TO** ALTITUDE SEVEN THOUSAND FEET.

... but is omitted from instructions or read back relating to flight levels:

BRITISH 12 ALPHA, CLIMB FLIGHT LEVEL 70.

The first message in an exchange relating to altitude or height should include the relevant QNH or QFE.

Headings

All reports, instructions and replies relating to headings should include the word 'HEADING'.

When a heading ends in zero, the word 'degrees' should be added:

WESSEX 10, TURN RIGHT HEADING 150 DEGREES.

... but not if the heading ends in any other number:

WESSEX 10, TURN RIGHT HEADING 155.

Headings are always transmitted using three figures with a zero at the beginning if necessary:

WESSEX 10, TURN RIGHT HEADING 030 DEGREES.

A heading of north is transmitted as THREE SIX ZERO (not ZERO ZERO ZERO), though cardinal headings (north, east, south, and west) may be transmitted as words:

EXAM 10, TURN RIGHT HEADING NORTH.

Pressure Settings

Pressure settings of less than 1000Mb have the word 'millibars' appended:

GOLF CHARLIE DELTA, DESCEND TO HEIGHT ONE THOUSAND FEET, QFE 999 **MILLIBARS**.

... while pressure settings greater than 1000Mb (and 1000 itself) leave it omitted:

GOLF CHARLIE DELTA, DESCEND TO HEIGHT ONE THOUSAND FEET, QFE 1001.

Time

UTC (Universal Time Coordinated – what used to be called Greenwich Mean Time) is the standard aviation time reference. Time checks are given to the nearest minute, and only the minutes of the hour are transmitted unless this would cause confusion:

time 0810 hours	MINUTE ONE ZERO ZERO EIGHT ONE ZERO	or, if the hour isn't obvious:
time 1523 hours	MINUTE TWO THREE ONE FIVE TWO THREE	or, if the hour isn't obvious:
time 1400 hours	ONE FOUR ZERO ZERO	

CALLSIGNS AND THEIR ABBREVIATIONS

Aeronautical Ground Station Callsigns

An Aeronautical Ground Station callsign is made up of two elements: a geographical location and a suffix indicating the type of service provided. For more details on this, *see* Chapter 2.

Aircraft Callsigns

An aircraft callsign may consist of one of the following:

- The registration letters of the aircraft:

  G-ABCD   GOLF ALPHA BRAVO CHARLIE DELTA.

- Type of aircraft (manufacturer, model or category) followed by its registration letters:

  Cessna G-ABCD   CESSNA GOLF ALPHA BRAVO CHARLIE DELTA.

  Helicopter G-ABCD   HELICOPTER GOLF ALPHA CHARLIE BRAVO DELTA.

- Company callsign, followed by either the aircraft registration letters, or the alpha numeric designation of that flight:

  British G-ABCD   BRITISH GOLF ALPHA BRAVO CHARLIE DELTA.

  British 12A   BRITISH 12 ALPHA.

- Authority callsign followed by a number particular to the aircraft commander:

  Exam 10   EXAM 10.

This last is used by CAA Flight Unit examiners (each of whom has their own number). A number of flight training organizations that provide training for the commercial flight tests use a similar system, substituting their company callsign for 'EXAM'.

Abbreviations

On initial contact, full callsigns must be used. Once communication has been established the ground station (not the pilot) may instigate the use of the abbreviated callsign, provided there is no possibility of confusion, and thereafter the pilot may also use the abbreviated callsign. Put another way, a pilot may not use the abbreviated callsign until the ground station has first done so.

Full Callsign	Abbreviation
G-ABCD	G-CD
N-12345	N-345
Cessna G-ABCD	Cessna CD
Helicopter G-ABCD	Helicopter CD
British G-ABCD	British CD
British 12A	No abbreviation
Exam 10	No abbreviation

The ground station may request that you go back to using full callsign if another aircraft with a similar callsign comes on frequency.

Up to now, in the phraseology examples, callsigns have been written out in full (e.g. GOLF ALPHA BRAVO CHARLIE DELTA). From now on, for the sake of brevity in the text, just the letters will be used (e.g. G-ABCD); however, the letters should still be voiced using the phonetic alphabet.

READ-BACK REQUIREMENTS

Pilots are required to read back certain elements of a radio message in order to provide a double check that the message has been received correctly and so allow the controller to correct it if not. Those elements that are required to be read back are the ones most likely to have serious consequences if misunderstood, and are summarised in the table below:

Read Back Required	Read Back Not Required
All level information: height altitude flight level transition level Headings Speeds All clearances: route/airways clearances approach clearances all runway clearances: land, take-off, enter, backtrack, cross, hold short Taxi instructions Runway in use Transponder settings Altimeter settings Radio frequencies Type of radar service VDF information	Everything else including: traffic information weather information, including wind speed and direction

A message containing required read-back elements must be read back:

G-CD, CLEAR LAND RUNWAY 27.

CLEAR LAND RUNWAY 27, G-CD.

A message containing no required read-back elements can be answered simply by using 'ROGER' (message received and understood), for a piece of information:

BRITISH 12 ALPHA, PREVIOUS AIRCRAFT REPORTED WINDSHEAR ON SHORT FINAL.

ROGER, BRITISH 12 ALPHA.

or 'WILCO' (I understand your message and will do as requested), for an instruction:

G-CD, REPORT WHEN YOU HAVE THE TRAFFIC IN SIGHT.

WILCO, G-CD.

If a message contains both required read-back elements and not-required read-back items, just read back the required bits and acknowledge the not-required bits with 'ROGER' or 'WILCO', as appropriate.

BRITISH 12 ALPHA, PREVIOUS AIRCRAFT REPORTED WINDSHEAR ON SHORT FINAL, CLEAR LAND RUNWAY 27, REPORT WHEN VACATED.

ROGER, CLEAR LAND RUNWAY 27, WILCO, BRITISH 12 ALPHA.

MESSAGE STRUCTURE AND REPLIES

Aircraft Initiating Contact with/Making Request to Ground Station

When initiating an exchange with a ground station, the callsign comes first followed by the message. On first contact the message format will be:

1. ATSU callsign,
2. aircraft callsign,
3. message.

FRAMPTON TOWER, G-ABCD, REQUEST START UP ON THE CLUB APRON.

Note use of full callsign on first contact.

On subsequent contact with the same ground station, the ground station callsign may be omitted, so the format will be:

1. aircraft callsign,
2. message.

G-CD, REQUEST TAXI.

Note use of abbreviated callsign (provided this has been used by the ground station first).

Aircraft Replying to Ground Station

When replying to a message or instruction from a ground station the read back/acknowledgment of the message comes first, followed by the aircraft callsign:

1. read back of required elements/acknowledgment,
2. aircraft callsign.

WESSEX 10, WIND 150 DEGREES 6 KNOTS, RUNWAY 09 CLEAR TAKE-OFF.

ROGER, CLEAR TAKE-OFF RUNWAY 09, WESSEX 10.

Chapter 4 Departure Procedures and Phraseology

Departure procedures will vary in detail from aerodrome to aerodrome, depending on local custom and circumstance. It is not possible to cover every conceivable situation here, so what follows are somewhat generic procedures. A pilot operating at an airfield at which they are not familiar should be able to get advice on local procedures from briefing facilities, local operators (such as a flying club) or handling agents, depending on the range of services available at the airfield.

We shall start by looking at those procedures and phraseologies used at an airfield with a full Air Traffic Control service. Differences appropriate to units operating with other levels of service are discussed at the end of the chapter.

RADIO CHECKS

A radio-check transmission may be made before flight (for the full procedure and readability scale, *see* Appendix II):

FRAMPTON GROUND, G-ABCD, REQUEST RADIO CHECK, 121.7.

G-ABCD, FRAMPTON GROUND, READABILITY 5.

Where more than one radio is fitted each needs to be tested individually: these are referred to as 'BOX ONE', 'BOX TWO', etc:

FRAMPTON GROUND, WESSEX 10, REQUEST RADIO CHECK BOX 1, 121.7.

Then select 'BOX TWO' and repeat the procedure, and so on.

AERODROME INFORMATION

Aerodrome information is usually collected before engine start. At larger airfields this will probably be provided by an ATIS broadcast (*see* Appendix IV). Where no ATIS is available the pilot can ask the ATSU:

FRAMPTON GROUND, G-ABCD, REQUEST DEPARTURE INFORMATION.

G-CD, FRAMPTON GROUND, RUNWAY IN USE 23, WIND 310 DEGREES, 14 KNOTS, TEMPERATURE PLUS 8, QNH 1005.

RUNWAY 23, QNH 1005, G-CD.

Note that only runway designator and QNH have been read back: the other pieces of information are not required read-back items.

START-UP

Usually there is a requirement to request engine start, but this is a particular area where there is a lot of variation in local practice. Generally, on main aprons permission will be required but light aircraft operating in specified areas (such as club parking areas) may be able to start up without calling ATC. If in doubt, err on the side of caution and request permission. Again depending on parking position and aircraft size, a marshaller or ground engineer may be required to be in attendance during start.

Aircraft position and aircraft type should be included in the request unless it is obvious that the controller will know where and what you are:

FRAMPTON GROUND, G-CD, CESSNA 172, REQUEST ENGINE START ON THE CLUB PARKING AREA.

G-CD, FRAMPTON GROUND, START APPROVED.

START APPROVED, G-CD.

Most light aircraft should have their avionics turned off during start to prevent electrical surges damaging the equipment, so if you turned the radios on to request start, remember to turn them back off again before starting.

At ATIS-equipped airfields the ATIS designator should be included in the start request along with the QNH:

FRAMPTON GROUND, WESSEX 10, REQUEST ENGINE START ON THE WESTERN APRON, INFORMATION UNIFORM, QNH 1005.

WESSEX 10, FRAMPTON GROUND, START WITH THE MARSHALLER APPROVED.

START WITH THE MARSHALLER APPROVED, WESSEX 10.

'START WITH THE MARSHALLER' implies that start is approved only under the direction of ground marshalling staff.

TAXI INSTRUCTIONS

The taxi clearance will always include a clearance limit, this being the furthest point to which the aircraft may proceed without further permission. The ability to recognize and pick out the clearance limit from an R/T transmission is an important skill to develop.

FRAMPTON GROUND, G-CD, REQUEST TAXI.

The clearance limit may be one of the following:

- a designated holding point:

  G-CD, TAXI TO HOLDING POINT GOLF 1, RUNWAY 23.

- relating to a recognizable feature on the airfield:

  G-CD, TAXI TO HOLD ABEAM THE FUEL FARM.

- and may include a specific routing to the clearance limit:

  G-CD, TAXI TO HOLDING POINT GOLF 1, RUNWAY 23, VIA TAXIWAY ZULU AND YANKEE.

Since all these are clearances they are all required to be read back:

TAXI TO HOLDING POINT GOLF ONE, RUNWAY 23, G-CD.

TAXI TO HOLD ABEAM THE FUEL FARM, G-CD.

TAXI TO HOLDING POINT GOLF 1, RUNWAY 23, VIA TAXIWAY ZULU AND YANKEE, G-CD.

Alternatively, if the controller wishes you to remain stationary (or if already taxiing, wants you to stop), he will use the phrase:

BRITISH 12 ALPHA, HOLD POSITION.

This is in effect a clearance where the clearance limit is your present position, and so must be read back:

HOLD POSITION, BRITISH 12 ALPHA.

Local procedure may require the destination to be included in the request to taxi, and QNH may be included in the instructions from the controller if he has not already had confirmation that the pilot has this information:

FRAMPTON GROUND, G-CD, REQUEST TAXI FOR VFR DEPARTURE TO HENFIELD.

G-CD, TAXI TO HOLDING POINT GOLF 1, RUNWAY 23, QNH 1005.

CONDITIONAL CLEARANCES

A conditional clearance is where you are cleared to do something after something else has happened:

BRITISH 12 ALPHA, AFTER THE AIRBUS ON SHORT FINALS, ENTER AND LINE UP 23.

Note the constituent parts and order of the clearance:

- callsign ('BRITISH 12 ALPHA');
- the condition ('AFTER');
- the subject of the condition ('THE AIRBUS ON SHORT FINALS'); and
- the clearance ('ENTER AND LINE UP TWO THREE').

A conditional clearance should be read back in the same order:

AFTER THE AIRBUS ON SHORT FINALS, ENTER AND LINE UP 23, BRITISH 12 ALPHA.

A conditional clearance should only be issued if both the controller and pilot can see the aircraft or vehicles involved. If you can't see the 'subject of the condition', tell the controller and refuse the clearance.

CHANGING FREQUENCY

If a separate Ground and Tower frequency are in use, control is usually passed from one to the other at, or shortly before, the final holding point before the runway:

G-CD, CONTACT FRAMPTON TOWER 119.250.

CONTACT FRAMPTON TOWER 119.250, G-CD.

FRAMPTON TOWER, G-ABCD, TAXIING HOLDING POINT GOLF 1, RUNWAY 23.

Note use of full callsign since this is the first call on a new frequency.

G-CD, FRAMPTON TOWER, CONTINUE TAXI, HOLD GOLF 1, REPORT READY FOR DEPARTURE.

HOLD GOLF 1, WILCO, G-CD.

It is particularly important to be aware of the clearance limit approaching an active runway. In the above exchange the controller has reiterated the clearance limit, previously given by the ground controller, by the phrase 'HOLD GOLF ONE', but had he not done so it is still the pilot's responsibility to be aware of the clearance limit. If in doubt, ask!

DEPARTURE/ROUTE CLEARANCES AND INSTRUCTIONS

These are issued at airfields within controlled airspace, where aircraft operating VFR are expected to follow specific departure routes indicated by reference to notified 'Visual Reference Points' (which are marked on the 1:5,000,000 charts).

The issue of a departure clearance does not constitute a clearance to take off.

A departure clearance may be quite complicated, and good airmanship dictates you write it down, so the controller may ask if you are ready to copy the instruction:

G-CD, ARE YOU READY TO COPY YOUR DEPARTURE CLEARANCE.

AFFIRM, G-CD.

Or if not ready:

NEGATIVE, STANDBY, G-CD.

If you have asked the controller to standby, you then need to inform him when you are ready:

READY TO COPY CLEARANCE, G-CD.

G-CD, WHEN INSTRUCTED, EXPECT A STANDARD VFR CASTLEHEAD DEPARTURE, NOT ABOVE TWO THOUSAND FEET, QNH 1005.

WHEN INSTRUCTED, EXPECT A STANDARD VFR CASTLEHEAD DEPARTURE, NOT ABOVE TWO THOUSAND FEET, QNH 1005, G-CD.

G-CD, READ BACK CORRECT, REPORT READY.

WILCO, G-CD.

Local departure instruction may 'stand alone', or be an amendment to a previous clearance. A local departure instruction does not itself imply permission to take off unless it is issued in conjunction with a take-off clearance:

G-CD, AFTER DEPARTURE CLIMB STRAIGHT AHEAD.

AFTER DEPARTURE CLIMB STRAIGHT AHEAD, G-CD.

A pilot may request a variation to the departure route if he considers he has good reason for doing so:

TOWER, WESSEX 10, AFTER DEPARTURE REQUEST EARLY RIGHT TURN DUE WEATHER.

WESSEX 10, EARLY RIGHT TURN APPROVED.

Again, approval of such a request does not itself imply permission to take off unless it is issued in conjunction with a take-off clearance.

READY FOR DEPARTURE

Pre-flight checks may be completed while stationary at the holding point, or during taxi according to the operating procedures of the particular aircraft type. Once these are completed the tower should be notified that the aircraft is 'READY FOR DEPARTURE':

G-CD, READY FOR DEPARTURE.

Note the use of the word 'DEPARTURE', not 'TAKE OFF'.

G-CD, HOLD POSITION.

HOLD POSITION, G-CD.

G-CD, LINE UP AND WAIT 23.

LINE UP AND WAIT 23, G-CD.

Note that clearance to enter and manoeuvre on the runway does not constitute clearance to take off, so enter the runway, line up and stop. Do not take off.

To 'backtrack' means taxiing down the runway in the opposite direction to the direction of take-off. A pilot who wishes to use a greater length of runway may request a backtrack, or the backtrack may be instigated by the controller for operational reasons, such as wake turbulence considerations – an aircraft starting its take-off run from the same position as the preceding aircraft does not have to wait as long as one starting from an intersection.

WESSEX 10, RUNWAY 23, LINE UP AND WAIT.

REQUEST BACKTRACK, WESSEX 10.

WESSEX 10, ROGER, ENTER, BACKTRACK, LINE UP AND WAIT 23.

ENTER, BACKTRACK AND LINE UP AND WAIT 23, WESSEX 10.

Should you be instructed to enter an active runway (or even take off) before being ready for take-off, inform the controller.

G-CD, LINE UP AND WAIT 23.

LINE UP AND WAIT 23, NOT YET READY FOR DEPARTURE, G-CD.

It is then up to the controller whether he allows you to proceed or cancels the clearance and instructs you to hold position.

Notwithstanding any clearance to enter or manoeuvre on an active runway, a pilot should maintain a good lookout and satisfy himself that it is safe to enter – controllers do occasionally make mistakes.

None of the clearances above include permission to take off. Note that up to now the phrase 'TAKE OFF' has not been used in any radio exchange. This is deliberate as 'TAKE OFF' is only used once permission to take off has actually been granted. A pilot only uses the phrase 'TAKE OFF' to acknowledge a take-off clearance, and may not use the phrase 'TAKE OFF' until the controller has done so first.

TAKE-OFF CLEARANCE

Permission to take off is indicated only by the use of the specific phrase 'TAKE OFF':

G-CD, WIND 310 DEGREES 14 KNOTS, RUNWAY 23, CLEARED TAKE OFF.

RUNWAY 23, CLEARED TAKE OFF, G-CD.

Sometimes the traffic situation requires that the take-off is completed expeditiously:

G-CD, RUNWAY 23, CLEARED IMMEDIATE TAKE OFF.

RUNWAY 23, CLEARED IMMEDIATE TAKE OFF, G-CD.

When the controller uses the word 'IMMEDIATE' it is expected that:

- an aircraft already lined up will commence take-off immediately; or
- an aircraft at the holding point will enter the runway, line up and commence take-off without stopping.

A controller may rescind a take-off clearance:

G-CD, HOLD POSITION, CANCEL TAKE OFF, I SAY AGAIN, CANCEL TAKE OFF, ACKNOWLEDGE.

HOLDING POSITION, G-CD.

... or instruct an aircraft that has already started its take-off run to discontinue take-off:

G-CD, STOP IMMEDIATELY, I SAY AGAIN STOP IMMEDIATELY, ACKNOWLEDGE.

STOPPING, G-CD.

Should a pilot decide to abandon take-off he will inform the ATSU as soon as reasonably possible:

G-CD, STOPPING.

Obviously once the situation is under control the ATSU should be informed why the take-off was abandoned and of the pilot's intentions.

In conditions of low visibility a controller may not be able to see that an aircraft has taken off and that the runway is therefore clear for the next movement. In these circumstances he will request that the aircraft reports when airborne:

BRITISH 12 ALPHA, RUNWAY 23, CLEARED TAKE OFF, REPORT WHEN AIRBORNE.

RUNWAY 23, CLEARED TAKE OFF, WILCO, BRITISH 12 ALPHA.

BRITISH 12 ALPHA, AIRBORNE.

CHANGING FREQUENCY

The flight will eventually be passed to the first en-route frequency, using the word 'CONTACT' when the flight details have been passed on to the next controller:

WESSEX 10, CONTACT FRAMPTON APPROACH 125.850.

CONTACT FRAMPTON APPROACH 125.850, WESSEX 10.

… or 'FREECALL', if they have not:

G-CD, FREECALL WINTERBOURNE RADAR 126.350.

FREECALL WINTERBOURNE RADAR 126.350, G-CD.

Having read back the instruction it is worth waiting just a couple of seconds before actually changing over, to give the controller a chance to correct you, in case you have misheard the frequency. It is not uncommon to hear a pilot read back a frequency incorrectly, and then when ATC transmit a correction, they receive no reply as the pilot has already gone.

At larger airfields the first frequency after departure is likely be another frequency within the same ATSU, such as 'Approach', in which case all that is necessary will be a brief message stating the departure route and level:

FRAMPTON APPROACH, G-ABCD, PASSING ONE THOUSAND FIVE HUNDRED FEET, CASTLEHEAD DEPARTURE.

Elsewhere the next frequency may be an entirely separate ATSU, and initial contact is dealt with in the next chapter. In either case, full callsigns should be used in the first transmission on the new frequency.

HELICOPTER-SPECIFIC PHRASEOLOGY

While the general rules of R/T are applicable to helicopter operations, the following specific phraseology and meanings also apply:

LIFT	Leave the ground to hover in ground effect, and remain in a stationary position.
AIR TAXI	Taxi at slow speed (less than 20kt) above the surface, in ground effect.
GROUND TAXI	(for helicopters with wheels) Taxi in contact with the surface.

If only the word 'TAXI' is used, the pilot may air taxi or ground taxi at his discretion.

HOLD	Come to a standstill. If ground taxiing, remain on the ground; if air taxiing, hover or touch down at the pilot's discretion, unless the controller says 'hover in the hold'.
HOVER IN THE HOLD	Remain airborne.
TAKE OFF YOUR DISCRETION	Used to authorize take-off when a helicopter is operating in a location not visible to the controller or areas other than the manoeuvring areas of the airfield. It is then up to the pilot to ensure it is safe to perform the manoeuvre.

AERODROME FLIGHT INFORMATION SERVICE PHRASEOLOGY

Since a Flight Information Service Officer (FISO) may issue instructions to an aircraft moving on the apron and other specified parts of the ground manoeuvring area, taxi instructions and read-back requirements will be the same as those described above. This also applies to helicopters that are air taxiing.

A FISO may relay clearances from an Air Traffic Control Unit, but must make clear from where the instruction originates:

G-CD, HENFIELD INFORMATION, I HAVE YOUR CLEARANCE.

GO AHEAD, G-CD.

G-CD, LONDON CONTROL CLEARS YOU TO JOIN CONTROLLED AIRSPACE ON TRACK CASTLEHEAD, CLIMBING FLIGHT LEVEL 60.

CLEARED TO JOIN CONTROLLED AIRSPACE ON TRACK CASTLEHEAD, CLIMBING FLIGHT LEVEL 60, G-CD.

A FISO may withhold permission to enter the runway:

G-CD, READY FOR DEPARTURE.

G-CD, HOLD POSITION, TRAFFIC TURNING FINAL.

HOLD POSITION, G-CD.

… and issue a clearance to taxi across a runway:

G-CD, CROSS RUNWAY 34 AT GOLF 2, REPORT VACATED.

CROSS RUNWAY 34 GOLF 2, WILCO, G-CD.

However, a FISO does not issue clearances to take off, or manoeuvre for departure on the runway, but instead uses the phrase 'AT YOUR DISCRETION' implying that it is the pilot's sole responsibility to make sure it is safe to perform the proposed action. The FISO will also pass relevant information, such as weather and traffic information, to aid the pilot's decision-making:

G-CD, READY FOR DEPARTURE.

G-CD, NO TRAFFIC KNOWN TO AFFECT, TAKE OFF AT YOUR DISCRETION, WIND 280 DEGREES 6 KNOTS.

While permission is not required, the pilot is still required to inform the FISO of what he intends to do, such as taking off:

ROGER, TAKING OFF, G-CD.

Note: not 'TAKE OFF AT MY DISCRETION'; pilots do not use the phrase 'at my discretion'.

… or backtracking:

ROGER, I REQUIRE TO BACKTRACK, G-CD.

G-CD, ROGER, TRAFFIC ON BASE, REPORT TAKING OFF.

ROGER, BACKTRACKING, WILCO, G-CD.

In the above reply 'ROGER' acknowledges the traffic information, 'WILCO' acknowledges the request to report taking off.

A FISO may request position reports, and such a request must be complied with:

G-CD, REPORT ENTERING THE RUNWAY.

G-CD, REPORT LINING UP.

G-CD, REPORT ABEAM CASTLEHEAD.

WILCO, G-CD.

AIR/GROUND COMMUNICATION SERVICE

A Radio Operator can only provide information to a pilot, such as weather and traffic information. He will not issue clearances or even use the phase 'AT YOUR DISCRETION'. He may relay clearances from an Air Traffic Control Unit, but must make clear from where the instruction originates. A relayed clearance must be read back in full.

Since there is no requirement for the Radio Operator to be able to see any of the aerodrome, all the information may be based on the reports of other pilots, so it is good airmanship to make position reports and advise him of your intentions so that he can pass the information on to any other traffic.

UNATTENDED AERODROMES AND SAFETYCOM

At airfields with no operating ATSU, a pilot may elect to make transmissions stating his intentions, and a listening watch should be maintained for other traffic doing the same, though no replies or acknowledgments are expected or required. Transmissions should be made on the frequency allocated to the airfield (e.g. on the Tower frequency outside hours of watch), and addressed to '(NAME OF AIRFIELD) TRAFFIC'.

Where there is no allocated frequency (and *only* where there is no allocated frequency) a common frequency called 'Safetycom' is available using 135.457MHz. Safetycom transmissions should only be made within ten miles of the aerodrome and at or below a height of 2,000ft agl, or 1,000ft above circuit height.

Transmissions at an unattended airfield are not mandatory so it is up to the pilot whether to make any or not; however where a pilot *does* elect to make such transmissions, the CAA specifies which transmissions should be made. During departure the specified transmission is lining up:

✈ LEYHILL TRAFFIC, G-ABCD, LINING UP FOR DEPARTURE 18.

... and may make such other calls as thought necessary:

✈ LEYHILL TRAFFIC, G-ABCD, TAXING FOR RUNWAY 18.

Use of Transponder During Departure

The transponder should be turned on at the relevant point in the aircraft checklist (after engine start in a light aircraft) and initially selected to standby.

If a specific code is allocated the transponder is usually selected to transmit (mode A or C or S) when entering the runway for departure, but it is increasingly common at large commercial airfields for this to be done at the start of taxi to aid ground movement control.

If no specific code is allocated, select 'standby', and then you may elect to squawk conspicuity (7000) once outside controlled airspace (*see* Appendix I).

Chapter 5 En Route Procedures and Phraseology

FREQUENCY CHANGING AND INITIAL CONTACT WITH AN ATSU

When changing to a new frequency, start off by listening out before making your initial transmission to avoid interrupting or 'stepping on' somebody else's transmission. If you receive no reply, wait a few seconds before repeating the transmission twice more. If there is still no response, you can probably assume that either the station is closed or you have got the wrong frequency, so the best thing to do is to go back to the previous frequency and request confirmation.

There are two basic formats of messages for making initial contact with a new station. In deciding which to use, you need to ask yourself whether the controller you are about to speak to knows you are coming and has your flight details, or whether your arrival on frequency will be completely unexpected. A clue to the answer to this question can be gained from the word the previous controller uses when instructing you to change frequency: an aircraft will be passed from one controller to another either by use of the word 'FREECALL' or 'CONTACT'.

Freecall

The instruction 'FREECALL', generally used for flights under VFR/outside controlled airspace, implies that your flight details have not been passed to the new controller, and he will not therefore necessarily have your flight details. Obviously these will need to be passed to him, but since he is not expecting your call, he needs an opportunity to pick up a pen and get a flight strip ready, so the first call should simply be a short message that includes the service required:

1. callsign of ATSU;
2. callsign of aircraft; and
3. request for the service required.

WINTERBOURNE RADAR, G-ABCD, REQUEST FLIGHT INFORMATION SERVICE.

Having got over the shock of your arrival on his frequency he will then request your flight details using the phrase 'PASS YOUR MESSAGE'. A useful mnemonic for the message contents is 'CAR PACER':

C Callsign
A Aircraft type
R Route – departure and destination
P Position
A Altitude (altitude/level/height)
C Conditions (VFR/IFR)
E Estimate for next waypoint
R Requests/intentions/any other information

G-CD, PASS YOUR MESSAGE.

G-CD, CESSNA 172, FROM FRAMPTON TO HENFIELD, OVERHEAD CASTLEHEAD, TWO THOUSAND TWO HUNDRED FEET MIDWOLDS QNH 1003, VMC, ESTIMATE BAGSTONE AT 15, SQUAWKING SEVEN THOUSAND.

This 'Initial Call' message format is particularly useful, and will be used as a template for numerous situations detailed in this book.

Contact

The instruction 'CONTACT', generally used for flights under IFR/inside controlled airspace, implies that your flight details have been passed to the new controller, sometimes called a 'handover', and he will therefore already have your flight details. In this case all that is required is a brief message stating callsign, level, and position or routing.

LONDON CONTROL, BRITISH 12 ALPHA, FLIGHT LEVEL 220 TOWARDS COMPTON.

POSITION REPORTING

A procedural Position Report contains the following items of information:

1. aircraft callsign;
2. position;
3. time;
4. level; and
5. next position/waypoint and ETA.

WESSEX 10, RANGEWORTHY AT 15, FLIGHT LEVEL 70, ESTIMATE FRAMPTON AT 36.

The point of the time element in the report ('RANGEWORTHY AT 15') is that, due to workload, it may not be possible to make the report exactly when at the reporting point, so the report may be made a short time later stating the time at which the point was passed.

Aircraft operating outside controlled airspace may not be operating on a route that will take them close to published reporting points, in which case the position element of the report can be made in relation to a recognizable geographical point or feature:

G-CD, TWENTY FIVE MILES SOUTHWEST CASTLEHEAD *etc.*

G-CD, EAST ABEAM HAWKSBURY *etc.*

LEVEL INSTRUCTIONS AND REPORTING

All reports, instructions, and replies relating to levels should include the word 'HEIGHT', 'ALTITUDE', or 'FLIGHT LEVEL' as appropriate.

For most practical purposes it is considered sufficiently accurate to make level reports to the nearest whole hundred feet, and the relevant pressure setting should be included if relating to a height or altitude:

G-CD, REPORT YOUR ALTITUDE.

FOUR THOUSAND FEET, MIDWOLDS QNH 1003, G-CD.

... though this would not be necessary when reporting flight levels:

BRITISH 12 ALPHA, REPORT YOUR FLIGHT LEVEL.

MAINTAINING FLIGHT LEVEL TWO HUNDRED, BRITISH 12 ALPHA.

An aircraft that is climbing or descending may be asked to report its passing level – the level it is actually climbing or descending through at the time of the report. The report should include the cleared level as well, if there is any doubt that the controller may be aware of this:

WESSEX 10, VERIFY YOUR PASSING LEVEL.

PASSING FLIGHT LEVEL 60, CLEARED FLIGHT LEVEL ONE HUNDRED, WESSEX 10.

In the above exchange the controller used the word 'LEVEL' which could be taken to mean height, altitude, or flight level. The pilots reply specified 'FLIGHT LEVEL' and so resolved any ambiguity, and would have given the controller the opportunity to come back had he actually wanted a report of altitude or height.

When dealing with any level instruction it is very important to maintain awareness of the type of level required, and have the correct altimeter subscale setting. If there is any doubt or ambiguity, ask!

The instruction to climb or descend means climb or descend and then maintain the stated level. Remember the word 'TO' is included if the instruction relates to an altitude or height:

G-CD, CLIMB TO ALTITUDE THREE THOUSAND FEET.

... but is omitted if the instruction relates to a flight level.

G-CD, CLIMB FLIGHT LEVEL 30.

All level instructions must be read back.

AIR TRAFFIC SERVICES OUTSIDE CONTROLLED AIRSPACE

As the name implies, Air Traffic Services Outside Controlled Airspace (ATSOCAs) are those services available to aircraft operating in class F and G airspace as opposed to controlled airspace (airspace classified A, B, C, D, and E). The services available are:

- Flight Information Service (FIS);
- Radar Information Service (RIS);
- Radar Advisory Service (RAS);
- Procedural Service; and
- Alerting (Emergency) Service.

FIS, RIS and RAS may be provided at the request of the pilot, but availability is subject to controller's work load, and so may be refused. Procedural and Alerting services are provided automatically by the controller as the situation warrants, and do not have to be requested by the pilot.

Flight Information Service

A non-radar service that provides information to aid the safe and efficient conduct of a flight, including:

- traffic information;
- weather;
- serviceability of navigation and approach aids; and
- aerodrome information.

Note:

- Traffic information will only relate to traffic participating in the service, or of which the controller is aware – you are responsible for your own 'lookout'.
- Since the service may be procedural only (i.e. based on the reports of participating aircraft), it can only be as good as the information the controller receives, so keep the controller informed of your flight's progress and any changes you make.
- If radar is available the controller may use it to help provide the service, and request participating aircraft to 'squawk', but allocation of a squawk code does not imply provision of any service, radar or otherwise.

Radar Information Service

A radar service that provides information (only) on conflicting traffic. This service is ideal for providing an additional 'safety net' for VMC operation.

Note:

- RIS provides information on other traffic only, not avoiding action, so you are responsible for maintaining your own separation.
- You must tell the controller before changing level or route.
- RIS may be used under all flight rules – VFR or IFR – and in all conditions – VMC or IMC – though a RAS (*see* below) is recommended for IMC.

Radar Advisory Service

A radar service that provides information on conflicting traffic, and advisory avoiding action to maintain separation. This service is ideal for IMC operation.

Note:

- RAS provides information on other traffic and avoiding action, but the avoiding action is advisory only and you may refuse it, but in that case you must inform the controller, and accept responsibility for maintaining separation.
- RAS is only available to flights operating under IFR (i.e. you must fly the appropriate quadrantal and maintain terrain clearance minima).
- It may be used in VMC or IMC. Remember that it is entirely legal for a non IMC/IR-rated pilot to operate under IFR outside controlled airspace provided that he maintains VMC. However, in that case, any avoiding action or other instruction that would lead to entering IMC must be refused.
- You must. tell the controller before changing level or route.

Procedural Service

A non-radar service providing separation between participating traffic based on position reports. Primarily used for IFR traffic when radar is not available, or when radar contact has been lost.

Alerting Service

Alerts the Search and Rescue services when a controller realizes or suspects that an aircraft is in trouble. Although a controller will provide this service on his own initiative when he believes it is needed, a 'MAYDAY' or 'PAN' call will bring the situation to the controller's attention more quickly.

Obtaining a Service

To obtain a service the pilot must make a request for service to the ATSU, stating the type of service required. The general layout of the message is the same as the 'initial call' message covered earlier:

WINTERBOURNE RADAR, G-ABCD, REQUEST RADAR INFORMATION SERVICE (or FLIGHT INFORMATION SERVICE, or RADAR ADVISORY SERVICE).

G-CD, WINTERBOURNE RADAR, PASS YOUR MESSAGE.

G-CD, CESSNA 172, FROM FRAMPTON TO HENFIELD, OVERHEAD RANGEWORTHY, TWO THOUSAND FIVE HUNDRED FEET MIDWOLDS QNH 1003, VMC, ESTIMATE BAGSTONE AT 15, SQUAWKING SEVEN THOUSAND.

Note the use of the 'initial call' format described above.

G-CD, IDENTIFIED, RADAR INFORMATION SERVICE.

RADAR INFORMATION SERVICE, G-CD.

It is important to note that merely requesting a service does not imply you are receiving it: you are only in receipt of the service once this has been agreed and confirmed by the controller.

Traffic Information

Information on conflicting traffic will usually contain the following elements:

- relative bearing (using the clock code);
- distance from the traffic;
- flight direction of conflicting traffic/relative movement; and
- relative speed, aircraft type (if known) and relative level of the traffic.

G-CD, UNKNOWN TRAFFIC RIGHT, TWO O'CLOCK, 4 MILES, CROSSING RIGHT TO LEFT, FAST MOVING.

ROGER, G-CD.

The controller will inform the pilot when the conflict no longer exists:

G-CD, CLEAR OF TRAFFIC.

ROGER, G-CD.

Radar Vectoring

When a pilot is receiving a RAS, the controller may issue heading instructions, a process referred to as radar vectoring:

G-CD, FLY HEADING 035.

FLY HEADING 035, G-CD.

Heading instructions must be read back. To issue instructions, the controller may need to know the heading the aircraft is on:

G-CD, REPORT YOUR HEADING.

HEADING 150 DEGREES, G-CD.

It is usually considered sufficiently accurate to report the heading to the nearest five degrees.

A controller may wish an aircraft to continue on the existing heading:

G-CD, CONTINUE PRESENT HEADING.

CONTINUE PRESENT HEADING, 150 DEGREES, G-CD.

The reply should include the heading.

Limited Service

Under certain conditions, such as reduced radar performance due to weather, terrain/technical issues, a high controller workload or traffic density, a limited service only may be available. In these circumstances the controller will issue a specific warning:

G-CD, WINTERBOURNE RADAR, APPROACHING THE BASE OF RADAR COVER TO THE WEST, LIMITED TRAFFIC INFORMATION.

ROGER, G-CD.

In any event, aircraft made of non-metallic materials, and slow-moving targets (balloons, gliders, microlights, etc.) may not show up on radar.

Termination or Alteration of Service

A controller may terminate or alter the category of service provided for technical or workload reasons. A pilot may terminate, or request alteration of the type of service provided:

G-CD, WINTERBOURNE RADAR, YOU'RE REACHING THE LIMIT OF MY RADAR COVERAGE, RADAR SERVICE TERMINATED.

ROGER, REQUEST FLIGHT INFORMATION SERVICE, G-CD.

G-CD, FLIGHT INFORMATION SERVICE.

FLIGHT INFORMATION SERVICE, G-CD.

You must always inform the controller before changing frequency.

WINTERBOURNE RADAR, G-CD, CHANGING TO HENFIELD INFORMATION 123.425.

G-CD, ROGER, RADAR SERVICE TERMINATED.

LOWER AIRSPACE RADAR SERVICE

LARS is the collective name for the provision of radar services (described above) to aircraft operating outside controlled airspace below Flight Level 95. Either RIS or RAS may be available, but provision of LARS is a secondary duty of the ATSU, and as such availability is subject to controller workload. Details of units providing LARS, such as frequencies, areas of coverage and hours of operation, can be found in the UK AIP.

MILITARY AERODROME TRAFFIC ZONE PENETRATION SERVICE

Active military airfields may be surrounded by a Military Aerodrome Traffic Zone (MATZ). Permission to enter is not mandatory, but because of the possible presence of fast-moving military traffic, civilian pilots are strongly recommended to seek a MATZ Penetration Service before doing so. (Note that a MATZ is not the same as the airfield ATZ. The ATZ within the MATZ *does* require permission to enter.)

Pilots requiring a MATZ Penetration Service are required to establish contact with the controlling ATSU when 15 miles or five minutes' flight time from the zone boundary:

HAWKSBURY RADAR, G-ABCD, REQUEST MATZ PENETRATION.

G-CD, HAWKSBURY RADAR, PASS YOUR MESSAGE.

G-CD, CESSNA 172, FROM FRAMPTON TO HENFIELD, OVERHEAD RANGEWORTHY, TWO THOUSAND FIVE HUNDRED FEET MIDWOLDS QNH 1003, VMC, ESTIMATE HORTON AT 15, SQUAWKING SEVEN THOUSAND.

Note use of the 'initial call' format again.

G-CD, MATZ PENETRATION APPROVED, MAINTAIN TWO THOUSAND FIVE HUNDRED FEET ON HAWKSBURY QNH 1004, REPORT LEAVING THE MATZ.

MATZ PENETRATION APPROVED, MAINTAIN TWO THOUSAND FIVE HUNDRED FEET ON HAWKSBURY QNH 1004, WILCO, G-CD.

While receiving a MATZ Penetration Service a pilot must inform the controller before changing level or heading, and is expected to comply with any instructions issued.

DANGER AREAS

A danger area may have available a nominated ATSU able to provide a service to aircraft wishing to cross it. Details can be found in the UK AIP or on the 1:500,000 chart. Where available the service will be one of the following.

Danger Area Crossing Service (DACS), which may be able to provide a clearance to cross the danger area under a FIS or RIS. The clearance issued is only valid in relation to danger activity and does not necessarily provide separation from other traffic in the area.

Danger Area Activity Information Service (DAAIS), providing information on activity within the area that allows the pilot to make up his own mind if it is safe to cross.

On initial contact, the standard 'initial call' format should be used, stating the service required and the name or number of the danger area in question:

HAWKSBURY RADAR, G-ABCD, REQUEST DANGER AREA CROSSING SERVICE (or DANGER AREA ACTIVITY INFORMATION SERVICE), DANGER AREA 123.

If it is not possible to contact the nominated ATSU, or otherwise verify the status of the danger area, you must assume it is active and stay out.

FLIGHT IN A CONTROL ZONE

There is an absolute legal requirement to obtain permission from the controlling ATSU before entering an active control zone. The logical implication of this is that until a clearance to enter the zone has been received you must stay out, and indeed such permission may be withheld if there is good reason. Having said that, most controllers are extremely helpful, and in practice permission to enter and transit a control zone is rarely refused absolutely.

There is nothing mysterious about flight in a control zone, and when route planning there is no particular need to avoid these areas of controlled airspace, but it would be prudent to have alternatives planned for the rare occasion when permission is not granted.

The first order of business is to establish contact while still outside controlled airspace, again using standard 'initial call' message format:

WINTERBOURNE APPROACH, G-ABCD, REQUEST ZONE TRANSIT.

G-CD, WINTERBOURNE APPROACH, PASS YOUR MESSAGE.

G-CD, CESSNA 172, FROM FRAMPTON TO HENFIELD, 15 MILES WEST OF HORTON, TWO THOUSAND FIVE HUNDRED FEET MIDWOLDS QNH 1003, VMC, ESTIMATE ZONE BOUNDARY AT 35, SQUAWKING SEVEN THOUSAND, REQUEST ZONE TRANSIT HORTON TO RANGEWORTHY.

Note that just making the request does not constitute clearance to enter the zone – until clearance is issued stay out.

The clearance, when issued, may contain instructions regarding level and routing, and since it is a clearance must be read back exactly:

G-CD, IDENTIFIED, CLEARED TO TRANSIT THE WINTERBOURNE CONTROL ZONE FROM HORTON TO RANGEWORTHY AT TWO THOUSAND FIVE HUNDRED FEET, WINTERBOURNE QNH 997 MILLIBARS.

CLEARED TO TRANSIT THE WINTERBOURNE CONTROL ZONE FROM HORTON TO RANGEWORTHY AT TWO THOUSAND FIVE HUNDRED FEET, WINTERBOURNE QNH 997 MILLIBARS, G-CD.

Once in controlled airspace all instructions and clearances must be complied with. That said, nothing in an instruction or clearance should force a pilot to enter conditions that he is not rated for, or otherwise able to fly in safely. If, for whatever reason, it is not possible to comply with an instruction, the controller must be informed.

G-CD, CLIMB TO ALTITUDE FOUR THOUSAND FIVE HUNDRED FEET.

UNABLE COMPLY, CLIMB WILL TAKE ME INTO IMC, G-CD.

G-CD, ROGER, MAINTAIN PRESENT ALTITUDE.

MAINTAIN PRESENT ALTITUDE, G-CD.

AIRBORNE FLIGHT PLANS

A flight plan may be filed by an aircraft in flight stating:

1. aircraft callsign;
2. aircraft type;
3. position and heading;
4. level and flight conditions;
5. departure aerodrome;
6. ETA at the proposed entry point of controlled airspace;
7. route and destination;
8. true airspeed; and
9. requested level in the airway or advisory route.

Since this message is relatively lengthy, it is recommended that airborne flight plans are filed on the Flight Information Service frequency.

SPECIAL VFR

Special VFR allows a pilot to operate visually under special instructions from the ATSU when compliance with IFR would otherwise be required. One use of such a clearance might be to allow a non-instrument-rated pilot to fly (in suitable conditions) in class A airspace, or in a control zone at night. An additional advantage is that while operating under a Special VFR clearance you are exempted from the 1,500ft rule (but not the land-clear requirements) of the low-flying regulations.

While a flight plan is not required, when requesting a SVFR clearance the ATSU should be informed of:

1. aircraft callsign;
2. aircraft type;
3. intentions; and
4. ETA at the proposed entry point of controlled airspace.

While operating under special VFR a pilot must:

- comply with any instructions given by the ATSU;
- remain clear of cloud and in sight of the surface;
- fly within the privileges of his licence;
- maintain terrain clearance, and comply with the low-flying regulations (except as exempted above); and
- remain clear of any ATZs within the controlled airspace, unless specifically cleared to enter.

VHF DIRECTION FINDING (VDF)

When an aircraft transmits, a suitably equipped ground station can determine the direction from which the signal came. This provides a 'position line', but not a 'position fix' as it is not possible to tell how far along the line the signal originated. Therefore, in order to produce a fix the VDF bearing has to be supplemented by further navigational information, which could be another VDF bearing from a different station.

The use of VDF has now been largely supplanted by radar and other navigation aids, but those stations still able to provide the service are listed in the UK AIP (AD section).

It is possible for the pilot to request the information to be supplied in a number of ways by using the appropriate 'Q code':

QDM Magnetic track to the station.
QDR Magnetic bearing of the aircraft from the station.
QTE True bearing of the aircraft from the station. Alternatively a QTE may be requested by substituting the phrase 'TRUE BEARING' for 'QTE'.

The accuracy of the VDF information is graded according to the following scale:

Class A Accuracy within +/–20°.
Class B Accuracy within +/–50°.
Class C Accuracy within +/–100°.
Class D Accuracy less than +/–100°.

A transmission for VDF consists of:

1. VDF station callsign;
2. full aircraft callsign;
3. the request; and
4. full callsign of the aircraft – to lengthen the transmission in order to allow the controller to register the DF information on his instruments.

✈ WINTERBOURNE APPROACH, G-ABCD, REQUEST QTE (or TRUE BEARING), G-ABCD.

G-ABCD, WINTERBOURNE APPROACH, QTE 050, CLASS BRAVO.

QTE 050, CLASS BRAVO, G-ABCD.

If the transmission was not sufficiently long to allow the bearing to be registered, the controller may request the aircraft to 'TRANSMIT FOR DF'.

G-CD, TRANSMIT FOR DF.

TRANSMITTING FOR DF, TRANSMITTING FOR DF, G-ABCD.

Homing Procedure

One of the main uses of VDF is to find your way to the airfield that is providing the DF service. DF is particularly suited to this as there is no need to know the exact distance from the station for the technique to work. The procedure is known as 'homing' and is especially useful if 'uncertain of position'. For this purpose the magnetic track to the station (QDM) is the most useful form of DF information.

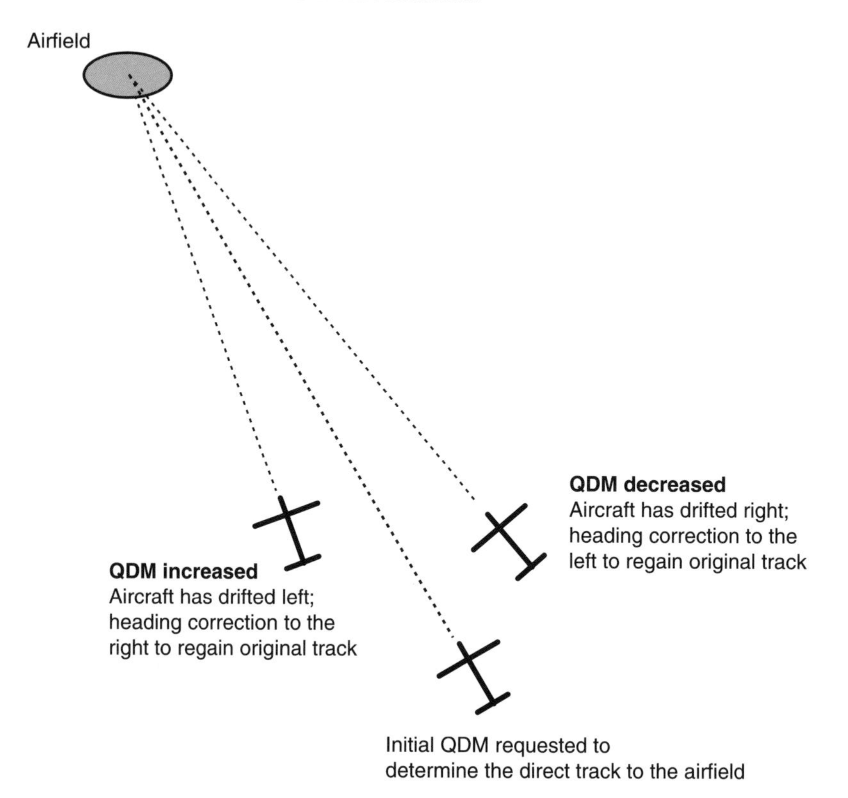

Homing with QDM.

The pilot will start by requesting a QDM but, as this does not take account of wind, the pilot must make a drift correction to the QDM to come up with an initial heading to steer to maintain the desired track. From then on QDM requests are made at approximately one-minute intervals to assess maintenance of track, and allow corrections as necessary:

The frequency of QDM requests should be increased as the airfield is approached. The QDMs will then change direction by 180 degrees as the airfield is reached and overflown.

Chapter 6 Arrival and Circuit Procedures and Phraseology

As with departures, arrival procedures will vary from aerodrome to aerodrome. This chapter follows the same general layout as that on departures, in that we start by looking at those procedures used at an airfield with a full Air Traffic Control service, and deal with differences appropriate to other types of ATSU later on in the chapter.

INITIAL CONTACT AND ZONE ENTRY

When approaching an airfield situated in controlled airspace, it is an absolute requirement to obtain entry clearance from the controlling ATSU before entering its control zone or area. The same holds true for Aerodrome Traffic Zones outside controlled airspace where an Air Traffic Control service is established. Merely making contact with the ATSU does not mean you have permission to enter.

☠ Until a specific entry clearance has been received you must stay outside.

At larger airfields, initial contact will probably be on the Approach frequency, who will then instruct you to contact other controllers at the appropriate time. At smaller units there may only be a Tower controller who will deal with the whole arrival from initial contact to shutdown.

The entry process is facilitated if initial contact is made a reasonable amount of time before the ATZ – or boundary of controlled airspace – is reached, otherwise it will be necessary to perform some sort of delaying manoeuvre, such as a hold or orbit. Obviously any such manoeuvre must be performed outside the controlled airspace boundary.

If the controller is not expecting your arrival (i.e. you are neither being 'handed over' by the previous controller, nor operating under a flight plan), use the standard 'initial call' message format. Here the initial request is for 'JOINING INSTRUCTIONS', a phrase that indicates to the controller that you wish to join the aerodrome traffic pattern and make an approach:

FRAMPTON APPROACH, G-ABCD, REQUEST JOINING INSTRUCTIONS.

G-CD, FRAMPTON APPROACH, PASS YOUR MESSAGE.

G-CD, CESSNA 172, FROM HENFIELD TO FRAMPTON, APPROACHING CASTLEHEAD, TWO THOUSAND FEET MIDWOLDS QNH 1003, VMC, ESTIMATE CASTLEHEAD AT 35, SQUAWKING SEVEN THOUSAND.

If the controller does know you are coming (i.e. the flight is being 'handed over' from the previous controller, or is operating under a flight plan), and therefore already has the flight details, the simplified form of message can be used. This format could also be appropriate when returning to the home airfield after a booked local flight, as the controller will be expecting your return, and will probably have kept the flight strip open.

FRAMPTON APPROACH, WESSEX 10, TWO THOUSAND FEET MIDWOLDS QNH 1003, APPROACHING CASTLEHEAD, INFORMATION PAPA RECEIVED, REQUEST JOINING INSTRUCTIONS.

Where an ATIS broadcast is available and has been received this should be acknowledged. In the transmission above the pilot has indicated this by use of the phrase 'INFORMATION PAPA RECEIVED'.

JOINING INSTRUCTIONS AND PROCEDURES

If no circuit direction is specified in the joining instructions you can assume a left-hand pattern (since the standard circuit direction is left hand). However, where the pattern is either right hand or variable, the controller should tell you. If in doubt, ask!

Larger airfields will generally expect aircraft operating under VFR to enter their airspace via set routes that are indicated by reference to notified 'Visual Reference Points', and then make a direct join to the circuit at the appropriate point. Entry instructions are clearances and so must be read back:

G-CD, FRAMPTON APPROACH, CLEARED TO ENTER CONTROLLED AIRSPACE, STANDARD CASTLEHEAD VFR ARRIVAL, JOIN LEFT HAND DOWNWIND RUNWAY 23, QFE 997 MILLIBARS.

CLEARED TO ENTER CONTROLLED AIRSPACE, STANDARD CASTLEHEAD VFR ARRIVAL, JOIN LEFT HAND DOWNWIND RUNWAY 23, QFE 997 MILLIBARS, G-CD.

It is particularly important to maintain an awareness of your clearance limit during arrival. In the above example a report would have to be made at or just before the downwind position, to get further instructions before proceeding.

The alternative type of arrival, more common at smaller airfields, is the standard overhead join:

1. route to the overhead at 2,000ft QFE;
2. if time is needed for orientation, take up an orbit in the overhead in the same direction as the circuit pattern;
3. when ready, descend on the 'dead side' (the opposite side of the active runway to the circuit pattern) to reach circuit height when crossing the upwind end of the runway;
4. remaining at circuit height, route to the downwind position to join the circuit.

Any variance from this standard pattern should be notified by the controller.

G-CD, FRAMPTON TOWER, JOIN OVERHEAD, TWO THOUSAND FEET, RUNWAY 23 RIGHT HAND, QFE 997 MILLIBARS.

JOIN OVERHEAD, TWO THOUSAND FEET, RUNWAY 23 RIGHT HAND, QFE 997 MILLIBARS, G-CD.

The pilot should then make position reports in accordance with local procedures or as requested by the controller:

G-CD, OVERHEAD.

G-CD, DEAD SIDE DESCENDING.

CIRCUIT CALLS

Similarly, once in the circuit, calls are made at a number of standard positions:

G-CD, DOWNWIND.

G-CD, BASE.

G-CD, FINAL.

Unless a pilot informs him otherwise, a controller will, not unreasonably, assume an inbound aircraft intends to land. If however the pilot wants some

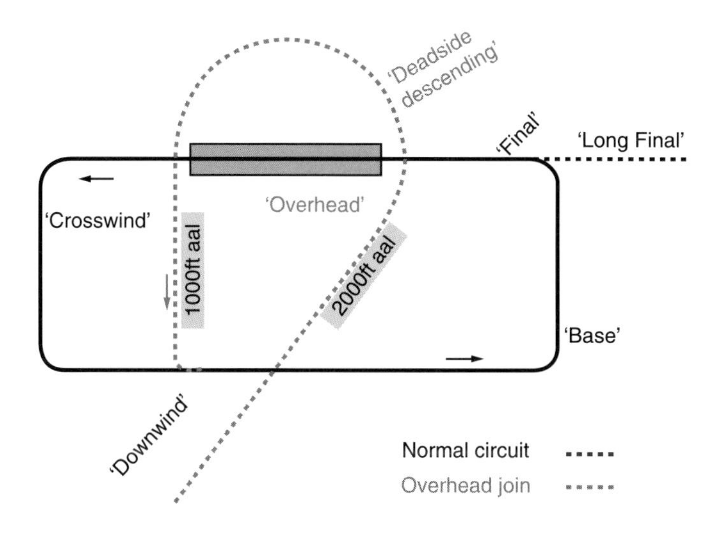

Position of calls in the circuit and overhead join.

other outcome from the approach he will need to request it, and this is usually combined with the 'DOWNWIND' call:

G-CD, DOWNWIND, REQUEST TOUCH AND GO.

WESSEX 10, DOWNWIND, REQUEST LOW APPROACH AND GO AROUND.

At this point the controller may only acknowledge the request, the actual clearance for the requested manoeuvre being issued once the aircraft has reported final.

Similarly if an aircraft that has been carrying out circuit practice now wishes to land it will help the controller plan traffic flow if he is informed of this:

G-CD, DOWNWIND TO LAND.

For spacing and in order to coordinate traffic a controller may ask an aircraft to report before proceeding to the next part of the circuit:

G-CD, REPORT BEFORE TURNING BASE.

REPORT BEFORE TURNING BASE, G-CD.

This effectively has become the clearance limit, in this case the end of the downwind leg before the turn on to base is started, and the pilot will have to report at this position before continuing.

G-CD, READY FOR LEFT BASE.

G-CD, CONTINUE TO FINAL.

Clearance to continue may depend on being able to see and maintain separation with other traffic:

G-CD, TRAFFIC IS A SENECA ON A 4 MILE FINAL, REPORT WHEN YOU HAVE THE TRAFFIC IN SIGHT.

VISUAL WITH THE SENECA, G-CD.

G-CD, CONTINUE INBOUND, REPORT FINAL NUMBER 2 TO THE SENECA ON A THREE AND A HALF MILE FINAL.

Here the clearance to continue to final is dependent on the other traffic. Since the traffic has become part of the clearance, the traffic details must be included in the read back:

CONTINUE INBOUND, REPORT FINAL NUMBER 2 TO THE SENECA ON A THREE AND A HALF MILE FINAL, G-CD.

It is the pilot's responsibility to maintain his assigned position in relation to other traffic in the pattern.

Alternatively the controller may request a delaying manoeuvre, such as extending the downwind leg:

G-CD, EXTEND DOWNWIND TO REPORT FINAL NUMBER 2 TO THE SENECA ON A 5 MILE FINAL.

EXTEND DOWNWIND TO REPORT FINAL NUMBER 2 TO THE SENECA, G-CD.

or an orbit:

G-CD, ORBIT RIGHT AT THE END OF THE DOWNWIND LEG, REPORT WHEN YOU HAVE THE TRAFFIC IN SIGHT.

ORBIT RIGHT AT THE END OF THE DOWNWIND LEG, WILCO, G-CD.

The instruction 'ORBIT' means continue orbiting until told to do otherwise. The controller may state the direction of the orbit, but orbits are nearly always carried out away from the runway (i.e. left-hand circuit = right-hand orbit).

WAKE TURBULENCE SEPARATION

Large aircraft produce wake vortices that can have a significant effect on following aircraft. Generally speaking the larger the preceding aircraft, and the smaller the one following, the greater the effect will be. Guidelines on the minimum separation for different aircraft types have been developed, and the recommended spacing should be passed to the pilot:

WESSEX 10, CONTINUE INBOUND, REPORT FINAL NUMBER 2 TO THE 737 ON A THREE AND A HALF MILE FINAL, CAUTION VORTEX WAKE, RECOMMENDED SPACING 4 MILES.

It is then up to the pilot to maintain safe separation. Remember that the spacing is only a recommendation, which a pilot may increase at his discretion. If a pilot becomes unhappy with his spacing he may request a delaying manoeuvre:

WESSEX 10, REQUEST ONE ORBIT RIGHT FOR SPACING.

WESSEX 10, ORBIT APPROVED.

FINAL APPROACH AND LANDING

At some point during approach the flight will be instructed to contact the Tower, as it is always the tower controller that has responsibility for issuing the landing clearance. Once established on the final approach track the pilot should report 'FINAL', or 'LONG FINAL' if more than 4 (but less than 8) miles from the threshold. (The phrase 'SHORT FINAL' has no official approval or meaning.)

G-CD, FINAL.

G-CD, RUNWAY 23, CLEARED TO LAND, SURFACE WIND 310 14 KNOTS.

RUNWAY 23, CLEARED TO LAND, G-CD.

If an aircraft reports final when the runway is still obstructed, but the controller thinks that it will become available in time for the aircraft to land, he may instruct the aircraft to continue the approach:

G-CD, CONTINUE APPROACH.

CONTINUE APPROACH, G-CD.

The instruction to continue the approach does not constitute clearance to land. Hopefully a landing clearance will be issued a short time later once the runway is clear.

An aircraft may be cleared to land before the preceding aircraft has cleared the runway, by use of the phrase 'LAND AFTER', under certain very specific circumstances:

- long enough runway to allow safe separation;
- daylight;
- the pilot of the landing aircraft is able to clearly see the preceding aircraft; and
- the pilot of the landing aircraft is warned of the presence of the preceding aircraft.

G-CD, RUNWAY 23, LAND AFTER THE SENECA, SURFACE WIND 310 14 KNOTS.

RUNWAY 23, LAND AFTER THE SENECA, G-CD.

It remains the absolute responsibility of the pilot of the landing aircraft to maintain safe separation. The pilot can refuse the clearance in the first place, or execute a 'Go around' if at any time he feels an unsafe situation is developing.

To expedite circuit training, an aircraft may wish to land, continue rolling while reconfiguring for take-off, and then take off without stopping. This is called a 'touch and go':

G-CD, CLEARED TOUCH AND GO.

CLEARED TOUCH AND GO, G-CD.

MISSED APPROACH/GO-AROUND

Under some circumstances it may be necessary to discontinue an approach to prevent an unsafe situation developing. The initial action in any missed approach is to establish the aircraft in a climb. Aircraft in the visual circuit will break to the dead side and climb to rejoin the circuit crosswind (though if the circuit direction is variable there is no dead side, so in that case maintain runway heading). Instrument traffic will carry out the published missed-approach procedure.

A missed approach may be carried out on the instructions of a controller, who will use the phrase 'GO AROUND':

G-CD, GO AROUND, I SAY AGAIN, GO AROUND, ACKNOWLEDGE.

GOING AROUND, G-CD.

... or be initiated by the pilot who will inform the controller using the phrase 'GOING AROUND':

G-CD, GOING AROUND.

In either circumstance the workload during a go-around is high, and the order of priorities for the pilot is Aviate – Navigate – Communicate. Any calls or replies can be left until the aircraft is established in a safe climbing configuration.

VACATING AND CLOSING DOWN

Instructions relating to leaving a runway use the word 'VACATE'. The phrase 'CLEAR OF' should not be used as it may be confused with a clearance such as a clearance to take off.

Some airfields have preferred turn-off points for different types of traffic, which may be notified in flight guides or be known to locally based traffic; otherwise the controller may specify a turn off point:

BRITISH 12 ALPHA, VACATE RIGHT ON FOXTROT.

VACATE RIGHT ON FOXTROT, BRITISH 12 ALPHA.

Controllers are usually very good at not passing instructions until the appropriate time, but in any event a pilot should wait until safe taxi speed is achieved before responding to any calls.

When a controller's ability to see is limited by weather or topography, he may request a pilot to inform him when he has vacated the runway:

BRITISH 12 ALPHA, REPORT RUNWAY VACATED.

WILCO, BRITISH 12 ALPHA.

RUNWAY VACATED, BRITISH 12 ALPHA.

Remember that the runway is not vacated until all of the aircraft has crossed the relevant holding point. If a Ground frequency is in operation then instructions will be passed to contact them, but a pilot should remain on the Tower frequency until the runway has been fully vacated.

Taxi instructions may specify a particular routing, and as for pre-departure taxiing it is important to recognize the clearance limit beyond which you must not proceed (in this case holding point Zulu 2):

BRITISH 12 ALPHA, TAXI VIA TAXIWAY GOLF AND ZULU, HOLD AT ZULU 2.

TAXI VIA TAXIWAY GOLF AND ZULU, HOLD AT ZULU 2, BRITISH 12 ALPHA.

The controller may simply specify the parking area and leave it up to the pilot how to get there if the traffic situation allows, and the route is obvious. If in doubt ask for clarification.

G-CD, TAXI TO THE LIGHT AIRCRAFT PARK, REPORT SHUTTING DOWN.

TAXI TO THE LIGHT AIRCRAFT PARK, WILCO, G-CD.

SHUTTING DOWN ON THE LIGHT AIRCRAFT PARK, G-CD.

In the exchange above the controller requested that the pilot 'REPORT SHUTTING DOWN' the engine(s). This is another areas in which there is a lot of variation in practice from airfield to airfield, depending on local custom, traffic and just how much of the airfield the controller is able to see. If this report is not asked for and you aren't sure if it's required, err on the side of caution and make the report.

HELICOPTER-SPECIFIC PHRASEOLOGY

Taxi phraseology has already been discussed in the chapter on Departure and is the same during arrival. The following additional phrases are appropriate to helicopter operations during landing:

TOUCH DOWN	Come into contact with the surface.
CLEARED TO LAND	Leaves the pilot free to choose whether to touch down or enter a low hover.
LAND YOUR DISCRETION	Used to authorize landing when a helicopter is operating in a location not visible to the controller, or areas other than the manoeuvring areas of the airfield. It is then up to the pilot to ensure it is safe to perform the manoeuvre.

MILITARY VISUAL CIRCUIT

The military circuit pattern differs somewhat from the civilian one: it tends to be oval in shape, with continuous turns from climb-out to the beginning of the downwind leg, and from the end of downwind to the threshold.

Since there is virtually no straight-in final, the final call is made at the end of the downwind leg immediately before turning base. Pilots of aircraft with retractable undercarriages should call 'GEAR DOWN' with the final call.

While a civilian pilot will communicate with a military ATSU on VHF, the military themselves predominantly use frequencies in the UHF band, so when calling a military unit you should allow the controller time to answer as he may be talking to military traffic on UHF; you may hear only one side of that conversation if his equipment is set to transmit on both UHF and VHF simultaneously, which can be a bit disconcerting. There are also a small number of differences of phraseology:

Military Term	Civilian Equivalent
Roll	Touch and go
Go around	Fly another circuit
Overshoot	Low approach and go around

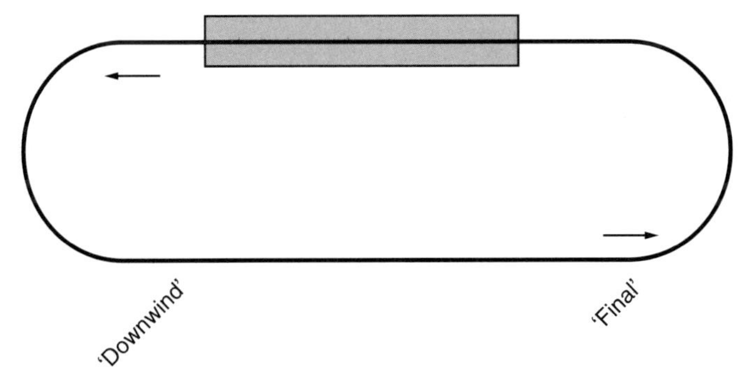

The military visual circuit.

AERODROME FLIGHT INFORMATION SERVICE PHRASEOLOGY

A Flight Information Service Officer cannot issue clearances or instructions to an aircraft in flight, but where an Aerodrome Flight Information Service is established it is a requirement to have established contact with the unit before entering the Aerodrome Traffic Zone.

The FISO will then be able to pass relevant information to the pilot, such as runway in use, circuit direction, weather, pressure settings, traffic information and any other essential aerodrome information.

Position reports within the traffic pattern are the same as for an airfield with ATC: remember that a FISO may request position reports, and such a request must be complied with.

A FISO does not issue clearances to land, but if he knows of no reason why the aircraft should not land he uses the phrase 'LAND AT YOUR DISCRETION', implying that it is the pilot's sole responsibility to make sure it is safe to perform the proposed action:

G-CD, FINAL.

G-CD, LAND AT YOUR DISCRETION, WIND 280 DEGREES 6 KNOTS.

The pilot should inform the FISO of his intentions:

LANDING, G-CD.

Note: not 'LAND AT MY DISCRETION'.

If, on the other hand, he is aware of information that may affect the pilot's decision he will provide this:

G-CD, ROGER, PIPER 28 AHEAD ON A 1 MILE FINAL.

G-CD, ROGER, AIRCRAFT LINING UP FOR DEPARTURE.

It is then up to the pilot to decide whether to continue the approach or to go around. While permission is not required, the pilot is still required to inform the FISO of what he intends to do.

Once the landing roll is complete a FISO may issue instructions to an aircraft moving on specified parts of the ground manoeuvring area and the apron, which must be read back.

AIR/GROUND COMMUNICATION SERVICE

A Radio Operator can only provide information to a pilot, such as weather and traffic information, so listen out for information, make position reports and advise him of your intentions so that he can pass the information on to other traffic.

UNATTENDED AERODROMES AND SAFETYCOM

At airfields with no operating ATSU, a pilot may elect at his discretion to make transmissions stating his intentions. Transmissions should be made on the frequency allocated to the airfield or, where no specific frequency is allocated, on the 'Safetycom' frequency: 135.457MHz. Transmission should be addressed to '(NAME OF AIRFIELD) TRAFFIC', and a listening watch maintained for other traffic doing the same.

Transmissions at an unattended airfield are not mandatory so it is up to the pilot whether to make any or not; however, where a pilot *does* elect to make such transmissions, the CAA specifies which transmissions should be made. During arrival the specified transmissions are:

Position and intentions when approaching the airfield:

✈ LEYHILL TRAFFIC, G-ABCD, TEN MILES NORTHWEST, JOINING OVERHEAD.

When downwind:

✈ LEYHILL TRAFFIC, G-ABCD, DOWNWIND.

On final:

✈ LEYHILL TRAFFIC, G-ABCD, FINAL.

And may make such other call as thought necessary (e.g. 'OVERHEAD', 'DESCENDING DEAD SIDE', 'BASE'.)

USE OF TRANSPONDER DURING ARRIVAL

If a specific code is allocated, the transponder is to remain selected to transmit (mode A or C or S) until vacating the runway, or until instructed otherwise, though it is increasingly common at large commercial airfields for it to remain on during taxi to aid ground-movement control.

Visual traffic with no specific code allocated should turn the transponder to standby when approaching the traffic pattern to prevent clutter on the approach controller's radar, and nuisance warnings for TCAS-equipped traffic.

Chapter 7 Emergency Procedures and Phraseology

While this is an R/T manual, it should be stressed that the order of priorities for a pilot at any time, but especially in an emergency, is:

1. **Aviate:** fly the aircraft and maintain flying airspeed. It is better to hit the ground in a controlled way while still flying than to stall in from altitude.

2. **Navigate:** away from danger and towards an airfield if possible.

3. **Communicate:** ATC may be able to help, and in the worst case get the rescue services to where you expect to come down.

Correct R/T protocol will help the controller to provide the necessary assistance, though it is accepted that in the stress of a real emergency situation some of the communication may be less than 'textbook'. For the exam, however, you will have to learn correct procedure.

DEGREES OF EMERGENCY

There are two recognized states of emergency:

Distress: a situation of being threatened by serious or imminent danger, and requiring immediate assistance. Prefixed by 'MAYDAY, MAYDAY, MAYDAY', a distress call takes precedence over all other R/T messages. (Morse code: SOS.)

Urgency: a situation concerning the safety of the aircraft, some other vehicle, or persons on board or in sight, but which does not require immediate assistance. Prefixed by 'PAN PAN, PAN PAN, PAN PAN', an urgency call takes precedence over all other R/T messages except distress calls. (Morse code: XXX.)

FREQUENCIES TO BE USED FOR EMERGENCY COMMUNICATIONS

In the first instance an emergency call should be made to the controller on the frequency currently in use. Any assigned transponder code should be maintained until instructed otherwise.

If not already in communication with an ATSU (or if communication has been lost) the call should be made on the international distress frequency 121.5MHz, (sometimes referred to as 'Guard'). If the aircraft is transponder-equipped, code 7700 should be selected with Mode C if available (*see* Appendix I), ideally before the R/T call is made. In the UK this call will be addressed to one of two Distress and Diversion (D&D) Sections, one located in the London Area Control Centre (ACC), the other in the Scottish ACC. Calls should be addressed to the London D&D section, callsign 'LONDON CENTRE', when south of 55° north, and to the Scottish D&D section, callsign 'SCOTTISH CENTRE', while north of 55° north, but don't worry if you can't remember which one to call: just call anyway.

Pilots are urged to make a call to air traffic services as soon as the safe progress of their flight is in any doubt, as an early intervention may prevent a situation becoming worse, and the situation may be easier for the controller to deal with. Also, while pilots appear to have a natural reluctance to declare a formal emergency, calls prefaced by 'MAYDAY' or 'PAN PAN' are much more likely to get an appropriate response than vague requests for assistance. Remember that an emergency can be downgraded or cancelled if the situation turns out to be not as serious as first thought.

Inexperienced pilots communicating with the D and D section, or with any military unit during an emergency, are encouraged to alert the controller to their lack of experience by prefixing their transmissions with the word 'TYRO'.

At larger airfields it may be possible to communicate directly with the Fire and Rescue Services on dedicated frequency 121.6. This facility is only to be used once the aircraft is on the ground.

EMERGENCY MESSAGE STRUCTURE

An emergency message should conform to the following format:

1. preface: 'MAYDAY, MAYDAY, MAYDAY' or 'PAN PAN, PAN PAN, PAN PAN';
2. callsign of ATSU – if known;
3. callsign of aircraft;
4. aircraft type;
5. nature of emergency;
6. intentions of pilot;
7. position/level/heading or, if lost, last known position;

8. pilot qualification (UK requirement only – may aid controller to plan a suitable course of action); and
9. other information, e.g. number of persons onboard (POB), endurance, etc.

MAYDAY, MAYDAY, MAYDAY, HAWKSBURY RADAR, G-ABCD, CESSNA 172, ENGINE FAILURE, ATTEMPTING FORCED LANDING, 4 MILES EAST OF RANGEWORTHY, PPL, 3 POB.

PAN PAN, PAN PAN, PAN PAN, LONDON CENTRE, WESSEX 10, PIPER AZTEC, UNSURE OF POSITION, SIX THOUSAND FEET, HEADING 060 DEGREES, LAST KNOWN POSITION OVERHEAD HENFIELD, CPL/IR/FLYING INSTRUCTOR RATING, NINETY MINUTES FUEL REMAINING.

An inexperienced pilot communicating with a D&D section or military controller is encouraged to use the prefix 'TYRO':

MAYDAY, MAYDAY, MAYDAY, HAWKSBURY RADAR, TYRO, G-ABCD, CESSNA 172, ENTERED IMC, CLIMBING TO MSA, PASSING TWO THOUSAND FEET, HEADING EAST, LAST KNOWN OVERHEAD BAGSTONE, PPL NO INSTRUMENT QUALIFICATION, 2 POB, 1 HOUR'S ENDURANCE.

UNCERTAINTY OF POSITION

As their name implies the D&D sections deal with aircraft in distress, but can also provide a position fix service to aircraft 'uncertain of their position'. Position fixing uses a combination of auto triangulation on 121.5, and fixes from other DF-equipped stations, and can take several minutes. Coverage over the UK is variable (e.g. more difficult over high ground), but is helped by higher altitude (greater than 3,000ft) and the availability of secondary surveillance radar, so climbing where possible and turning on your transponder are both good ideas.

Action When Uncertain of Position:

1. fly the aeroplane;
2. synchronize DI with compass;
3. turn onto required heading and orientate chart;
4. mark estimated DR position; and
5. attempt to establish position, reading from ground to chart.

If none of the above re-establishes your position, seek help from an ATSU. Initially this should be on the frequency in current use, but if they do not have the facilities to help, or if contact has been lost, it may be possible to request a 'Training Fix' on 121.5MHz (*see* below). If you have been unable to establish a positive fix for more than 15 minutes or so, then you are lost!

Action When Lost

1. fly the aeroplane;
2. squawk 7700; and
3. declare an emergency.

Provided that you are able to maintain flight within conditions that you are trained, rated and current to operate in, and there are no other problems, request assistance by making a 'PAN' (urgency) call to the D&D cells on 121.5. Climbing may increase radio range and assist radar identification.

If at any time deteriorating weather, impending nightfall, fuel state or any further problems preclude safe continuation of the flight, then the situation should be upgraded to 'MAYDAY' (distress) status.

EMERGENCY RELAY AND RESPONSIBILITIES OF OTHER AIRCRAFT

Upon hearing an emergency message all other stations on frequency should maintain silence until the situation is resolved, or until instructed otherwise by the station controlling communications.

The controlling station may transfer other aircraft to another frequency:

MAYDAY G-ABCD, ALL OTHER STATIONS CONTACT FRAMPTON RADAR ON 136.075.

No reply should be made to this message.

There is a general duty to provide any assistance of which you are capable that may be requested.

If when you hear an emergency message the station addressed does not reply, you may be able to assist by relaying the message, but make sure that it is clear that the message is being relayed and does not originate from yourself:

MAYDAY, MAYDAY, MAYDAY, HAWKSBURY RADAR, WESSEX 10, RELAYING INTERCEPTED MAYDAY TRANSMISSION FROM G-ABCD, I SAY AGAIN INTERCEPTED MAYDAY TRANSMISSION FROM G-ABCD, CESSNA 172, ENGINE FAILURE, ATTEMPTING FORCED LANDING, 4 MILES EAST OF RANGEWORTHY, PPL, 3 POB.

TERMINATION OF EMERGENCY COMMUNICATION

If a pilot feels the emergency situation has improved such that it no longer constitutes an emergency, a message can be transmitted cancelling the emergency, using the phrase 'CANCEL MAYDAY', or 'CANCEL PAN' as appropriate:

LONDON CENTRE, WESSEX 10, CANCEL PAN, POSITION RE-ESTABLISHED OVERHEAD HEATHROW, REQUEST THE FREQUENCY OF HEATHROW APPROACH.

... and in this case, perhaps the telephone number of a good aviation lawyer!

PRACTICE EMERGENCIES AND TRAINING FIXES

Training Fix

An aircraft wishing to confirm its position without carrying out a practice emergency may request a 'training fix' on frequency 121.5:

LONDON CENTRE, G-ABCD, TRAINING FIX, TRAINING FIX, TRAINING FIX.

G-ABCD, LONDON CENTRE, YOUR POSITION IS 10 MILES NORTH OF CASTLEHEAD.

A training fix is of a lower priority than Distress or Urgency transmissions, but takes precedence over 'Practice PAN' calls.

Practice PAN

For training purposes it is possible to make practice 'urgency' ('PAN PAN') transmissions to either the D&D cell on 121.5 or to your local ATSU. Start by listening out on frequency to make sure that a real emergency is not in progress, or that the unit is not too busy. The call should then be made prefixed by the phrase 'PRACTICE PAN' spoken three times.

PRACTICE PAN, PRACTICE PAN, PRACTICE PAN, HAWKSBURY RADAR, G-ABCD.

Acceptance of the 'Practice Pan' will be subject to workload and may be refused, but if accepted the controller will reply:

G-ABCD, HAWKSBURY RADAR, CONTINUE WITH PRACTICE PAN.

When carrying out a practice emergency it is perfectly acceptable to request 'diversion' to your intended destination so as not to disrupt your planned flight.

Care should be taken to ensure that the simulated urgency is not confused with the real thing.

HAWKSBURY RADAR, G-ABCD, CESSNA 172, SIMULATING UNCERTAINTY OF POSITION, THREE THOUSAND FEET, HEADING 345. LAST KNOWN POSITION WEST ABEAM WINTERBOURNE, PPL/IMC, 2 HOURS' ENDURANCE, REQUEST DIVERSION TO HENFIELD.

Only 'urgency' ('PAN') transmissions may be practised; simulated 'distress' ('MAYDAY') calls must never be made.

Squawk code 7700 must not be selected for practice emergencies.

RADIO FAILURE

In these security-conscious post-9/11 times, the authorities are likely to take a serious view of an aircraft (even a light aircraft) that inexplicably goes off the air near a sensitive installation, and in the UK most places will be near something sensitive. So if the frequency goes unusually quiet for a significant period, it is always worth asking for a radio check:

WINTERBOURNE RADAR, G-ABCD, RADIO CHECK, 126.350.

G-ABCD, WINTERBOURNE RADAR, READABILITY 5.

The full radio check procedure and readability codes are described in Appendix II.

If no reply is received, before jumping to the conclusion that you have a radio failure, it is worth making a few simple checks for basic procedural errors:

- Has the radio been turned off accidentally?
- Is the correct 'box' selected, and routed to the correct output (speaker or headset)?
- Is the volume set correctly? (Check using the squelch.)
- Have you set the correct frequency?
- Is the ATSU open and in range? If unsure try calling an alternative frequency such as the previous frequency, an en-route frequency, the D&D section (121.5), or another aircraft.

If you have checked and rectified the above items without success, it may well be that you do have a technical problem. Before adopting the radio-failure procedure, it may be possible to rectify the situation. Exactly what is possible will depend on the nature of the problem, the radio fit of the aircraft and the technical knowledge of the operator, but the following simple points are fairly universal:

- Check that the headset jacks are properly inserted.
- If more than one radio is fitted, change boxes.

- If a spare is available, change headsets.
- Check whether a PTT button stuck (which may be indicated by the transmission indicator being continuously illuminated on the radio set) – if so it may be possible to free it. This is a particularly problematic failure as, in addition to your own communication problem, your continuous transmission will also be blocking the frequency for others.

Some pilots carry a hand-held radio as backup, and of course a mobile phone may also work as a last resort, though this is a very unofficial method of communication. If none of the above steps restore communication, you do now need to adopt the appropriate radio-failure procedure:

1. Squawk 7600.
2. Transmit all messages twice, at the appropriate times on the appropriate frequency, preceded by the phrase 'TRANSMITTING BLIND' (in case the transmitter is still functioning).

From then on it depends on the type of airspace you are operating in (controlled or uncontrolled), your flight rules and conditions (VFR or IFR, VMC or IMC) and the extent of the problem (complete failure, or transmitter-only or receiver-only failure). The different rules for each condition are set out in the UK AIP, and are quite complex, so what follows is hopefully a slightly more digestible summary.

VFR/SVFR Outside Controlled Airspace

Remain in VMC, and outside controlled airspace, unless clearance to enter controlled airspace had already been given (SVFR remain outside even if cleared). Proceed to the nearest suitable airfield to land. Some airfields have local procedures that should be followed if known (e.g. if returning to home base), otherwise an overhead join is preferred. Look for, and obey, light signals (*see* below) from the ATSU, and any information provided by a signal square.

IFR Outside Controlled Airspace

If possible regain VMC and proceed as above. If conditions prevent this, an instrument let-down should be made at an airfield outside controlled airspace, as you may not enter controlled airspace unless clearance had already been received. Obviously there comes a point where, if the pilot considers himself to be in a distress situation (e.g. running low on fuel), the prohibition on entering controlled airspace may be ignored.

(S)VFR Inside Controlled Airspace

Maintain VMC, proceed to the last cleared waypoint, and then to the nearest suitable airfield to land as for VFR outside controlled airspace.

IFR Inside Controlled Airspace

Proceed as current flight plan to the appropriate designated navigation aid serving the aerodrome of intended landing. Maintain the last acknowledged cruising level to the point specified in the clearance, and thereafter the cruising level specified in the flight plan. Hold over the designated aid in order to commence descent at, or as close as possible to, the most recently received Expected Approach Time or, if no EAT has been received, as close as possible to the ETA indicated in the flight plan. Complete the published instrument approach procedure, and aim to land within thirty minutes from the ETA or EAT.

Individual airfields may have local procedures, which will be published in the relevant flight guides.

Receiver Failure

Transmit all messages twice preceded by 'TRANSMITTING BLIND DUE TO RECEIVER FAILURE' and proceed as detailed above, appropriate to flight conditions and airspace rules.

Transmitter Failure

Follow ATC instructions. It may be possible to establish a form of two-way communication by acknowledging/answering instructions by use of the ident function on the transponder:

G-ABCD, IF YOU READ THIS TRANSMISSION SQUAWK IDENT.

Alternatively, by responding to instructions to manoeuvre that are visible on radar:

G-ABCD, IF YOU READ THIS TRANSMISSION TURN LEFT HEADING 160 DEGREES.

If you are able to transmit carrier wave only, you can use the 'speechless code', which relies on the fact that depressing the PTT button produces an audible 'click'. If the callsign of the aircraft is unknown, the controller will address it as 'SPEECHLESS AIRCRAFT'.

The Speechless Code

Number of Clicks		Meaning
one short	•	affirm or acknowledge
two short	• •	negative
three short	• • •	say again or unable (to comply)
four short (Morse code h)	• • • •	initial alerting or request homing
two long (2 sec) (Morse code m)	– –	manoeuvre complete
one long, two short, one long (Morse code x)	– • • –	I have developed another emergency

Light Signals from an ATSU to an Aircraft

Light Signal	To an aircraft in flight	To an aircraft on the ground
flashing red light	do not land; airfield not available for landing	move clear of landing area
steady red light	give way to other aircraft, continue circling	stop
red pyrotechnic or flare	irrespective of previous instructions, do not land; await permission	n/a
flashing green light	return to aerodrome; await permission to land	you may move on the manoeuvring area and apron
steady green light	cleared to land	cleared to take off
flashing white light	land at this aerodrome after receiving steady green light, and then after receiving flashing green light proceed to parking area	return to starting position on the aerodrome

AVOIDING ACTION

Instructions including the term 'AVOIDING ACTION' are issued when the controller considers that an imminent risk of collision exists if action is not taken immediately:

BRITISH 12 ALPHA, AVOIDING ACTION, TURN RIGHT HEADING 120 DEGREES, POP UP TRAFFIC TWELVE O'CLOCK, RECIPROCAL HEADING, TWO THOUSAND FEET BELOW, CLIMBING.

Obviously an expeditious response to the instruction is required. Executing the required manoeuvre comes first, the reply can wait until the manoeuvre has been established or even completed:

TURNING RIGHT HEADING 120 DEGREES, BRITISH 12 ALPHA.

AIRPROX REPORTING

An AIRPROX report should be filed whenever a pilot considers that the distance between aircraft as well as their relative positions and speed have been such that the safety of the aircraft was or may have been compromised. Initially the call should be made to the controller on the frequency in use, unless the controller is too busy, in which case the report should be filed after landing. An AIRPROX report takes the following format:

1. the phrase 'AIRPROX REPORT';
2. aircraft callsign;
3. SSR code;
4. position of incident;
5. aircraft heading;
6. level (height, altitude, flight level);
7. altimeter setting;
8. aircraft attitude (climbing, descending, level or turning);
9. weather conditions;
10. date and time of incident (UTC);
11. description of other aircraft; and
12. description of incident (distance at sighting of other aircraft relative flight paths, etc.).

AIRPROX reports filed by R/T must be confirmed in writing within seven days.

INTERCEPTION BY MILITARY AIRCRAFT

Internationally agreed procedures exist to cover interception by a military aircraft. If intercepted, adopt the following procedures:

1. follow instructions given by the intercepting aircraft;
2. notify the ATSU on the frequency in use;
3. attempt to establish communication with the intercepting aircraft on 121.5; and
4. squawk 7700.

If instructions from any source (e.g. an ATSU) conflict with those from the intercepting aircraft, follow the instructions of the intercepting aircraft while seeking clarification from the ATSU.

Communication between intercepting and intercepted aircraft will be either by R/T or visual signal (*see* tables below).

Radio Communication During Interception

If communication in a common language is not possible, the following simplified R/T phraseology is used:

Phrases for Use by Intercepting Aircraft

Phrase	Pronunciation	Meaning
CALLSIGN	KOL-SA-IN	what is your callsign
FOLLOW	FOLL-LO	follow me
DESCEND	DEE-SEND	descend for landing
YOU LAND	YOU-LAND	land at this aerodrome
PROCEED	PRO-SEED	you may proceed

Phrases for Use by Intercepted Aircraft

Phrase	Pronunciation	Meaning
CALLSIGN	KOL-SA-IN	my callsign is
WILCO	WILL-KO	understood will comply
CANNOT	KANN-NOTT	unable to comply
REPEAT	REE-PEET	repeat your instruction
AM LOST	AM-LOSST	position unknown
MAYDAY	MAYDAY	I am in distress
HIJACK	HI-JACK	I have been hijacked
LAND (place name)	LAND (place name)	I request to land at (place name)
DESCEND	DEE-SEND	I require descent

Visual Communication During Interception

The following light signals are internationally agreed:

From Intercepting Aircraft

Signal	Meaning	Response
Takes up position ahead, rocks wings, turns slowly onto heading	You have been intercepted, follow me	Rocks wings
Abrupt breakaway – climbing turn through greater than 90°	You may proceed	Rocks wings
Circles aerodrome, lowers landing gear, overflies runway in the direction of landing	Land at this aerodrome	Lowers landing gear, lands

From Intercepted Aircraft

Signal	Meaning	Response
Raises landing gear while overflying runway between 1,000 and 2,000ft aal, continues to circle aerodrome	The aerodrome you have designated is inadequate	Re-intercepts (as above) and leads to another airfield, or 'You may proceed' (as above)
Regular switching on and off of all available lights	Cannot comply	Appropriate signal as above
Irregular switching on and off of all available lights	In distress	Appropriate signal as above

Chapter 8 Radiotelephony – Practical Application

So far we have looked at the component parts of R/T phraseology, and now we need to put them all together. Obviously it is not possible to cover every conceivable situation, but we will now look at a representative flight similar to the sort of scenario found in the Practical Communications Test.

The route our flight will follow (which can be traced on the southern 1:500,000 chart) is from Kemble to Bristol via a turning point overhead Henstridge, and the Cheddar VRP.

At Kemble:

✈ KEMBLE INFORMATION, G-ABCD, REQUEST RADIO CHECK 118.9.

G-CD, KEMBLE INFORMATION, READ YOU 5.

The ATSU has used the abbreviated callsign so you can too.

✈ ROGER, REQUEST AIRFIELD INFORMATION AND TAXI, VFR DEPARTURE TO BRISTOL, G-CD.

G-CD, RUNWAY 25, SURFACE WIND 270 8 KNOTS, QNH 1006. LEFT ON THE GRASS TAXIWAY, REPORT APPROACHING HOLDING POINT ALPHA 2.

Although from an Aerodrome Flight Information Service Unit, the above does *constitute a clearance as a FISO is permitted to pass instructions to aircraft operating on the apron and specific parts of the manoeuvring area.*

Maintain awareness of the clearance limit, in this case Alpha 2.

✈ LEFT TURN, TAXI VIA THE GRASS TAXIWAY TO HOLDING POINT ALPHA 2, RUNWAY 25, QNH 1006, G-CD.

G-CD, APPROACHING ALPHA 2.

G-CD, CONTINUE TO ALPHA 1.

CONTINUE TO ALPHA 1, G-CD.

At holding point Alpha 1:

G-CD, READY FOR DEPARTURE.

G-CD, HOLD POSITION, TRAFFIC ON A ONE MILE FINAL.

HOLD POSITION, ROGER, G-CD.

Once the traffic has landed:

G-CD, TRAFFIC IS A PIPER CHEROKEE JUST REPORTED DOWNWIND, TAKE OFF AT YOUR DISCRETION, WIND 270 6 KNOTS.

G-CD, LINING UP.

G-CD, ROGER.

G-CD, TAKING OFF.

Just south-west of the Kemble ATZ, approaching Malmesbury:

KEMBLE, G-CD, CHANGING TO LYNEHAM 123.4.

G-CD, ROGER.

Even though Kemble did not specifically ask for a report when leaving the frequency, you must always inform an ATSU before you change to another frequency.

Since the next frequency does not have your flight details, a full 'initial call' message will be required. However, don't launch into it straight away, as the controller is not expecting you and will need a moment to get a flight strip ready. Pass a short message, stating the service required, to alert him to your presence then wait until asked to 'pass your message'.

LYNEHAM APPROACH, G-ABCD, REQUEST ZONE TRANSIT.

Note use of full callsign again, as this is the first call on a new frequency.

G-CD, LYNEHAM, PASS YOUR MESSAGE.

LYNEHAM, G-CD CESSNA 172, FROM KEMBLE TO BRISTOL ROUTING VIA HENSTRIDGE, APPROACHING MALMESBURY, TWO THOUSAND THREE HUNDRED FEET COTSWOLD PRESSURE SETTING 1007, VMC, ESTIMATE MALMESBURY AT 15.

G-CD, ARE YOU TRANSPONDER EQUIPPED.

AFFIRM, G-CD.

G-CD, SQUAWK 4053 MODE CHARLIE.

SQUAWK 4053, NEGATIVE MODE CHARLIE, G-CD.

G-CD, IDENTIFIED 1 MILE NORTH OF MALMESBURY, CLEAR TO TRANSIT THE LYNEHAM CONTROL ZONE VIA THE OVERHEAD, CLIMB ON TRACK TO FOUR THOUSAND FEET LYNEHAM QNH 1006, REPORT PASSING THREE THOUSAND FIVE HUNDRED FEET.

CLEAR TO TRANSIT THE LYNEHAM CONTROL ZONE VIA THE OVERHEAD, CLIMB ON TRACK TO FOUR THOUSAND FEET LYNEHAM QNH 1006, REPORT PASSING THREE THOUSAND FIVE HUNDRED FEET, G-CD.

It is not uncommon for Air Traffic to clear an aircraft through their zone via the airfield overhead as this will keep the transiting traffic clear of the approach and climb-out paths.

PASSING THREE THOUSAND FIVE HUNDRED FEET, G-CD.

G-CD, ROGER, RADAR CONTROL, REPORT WHEN LEVEL, ADVISE AT ANY TIME IF UNABLE TO MAINTAIN VMC.

Even though under radar control, nothing in a clearance should force a pilot to enter conditions that he is not rated for, or otherwise able to fly in safely. In this case the controller has told you to let him know if you are unable to maintain VMC, but even if he hadn't you would have to do so, and if necessary refuse the clearance.

RADAR CONTROL, WILCO, G-CD.

LEVEL FOUR THOUSAND FEET, G-CD.

G-CD, ROGER, MAINTAIN, REPORT OVERHEAD.

REPORT OVERHEAD, G-CD.

G-CD, OVERHEAD.

G-CD, ROGER, CONTINUE YOUR PRESENT HEADING.

CONTINUE PRESENT HEADING, 150 DEGREES.

When instructed to continue a present heading, state the heading to the controller in the reply. In this case the heading ends in zero so the word 'degrees' is used.

G-CD, RESUME OWN NAVIGATION HENSTRIDGE.

OWN NAVIGATION HENSTRIDGE, G-CD.

ALL STATIONS, LYNEHAM APPROACH, QNH CHANGE 1005.

No reply is required for an all-stations broadcast unless specifically requested.

Abeam Calne:

G-CD, YOUR CURRENT TRACK WILL TAKE YOU CLOSE TO KEEVIL ACTIVE WITH PARACHUTING UP TO TWELVE THOUSAND FEET, STATE YOUR INTENTIONS.

REQUEST ROUTE EAST OF KEEVIL VIA DEVIZES, G-CD.

G-CD, ROGER, TURN LEFT HEADING 175, REPORT LEAVING CONTROLLED AIRSPACE.

In this case the heading does not end in zero so the word 'degrees' is omitted.

TURN LEFT HEADING 175, WILCO, G-CD.

LEAVING CONTROLLED AIRSPACE, G-CD.

G-CD, ROGER, OWN NAVIGATION DEVIZES, WHAT KIND OF SERVICE DO YOU REQUIRE OUTSIDE CONTROLLED AIRSPACE.

OWN NAVIGATION DEVIZES, REQUEST RADAR INFORMATION, G-CD.

G-CD, RADAR INFORMATION SERVICE, REPORT AT DEVIZES.

RADAR INFORMATION SERVICE, WILCO, G-CD.

G-CD, DESCENDING TO THREE THOUSAND FEET.

Outside controlled airspace you are able to choose your own actions (such as descending to 3,000ft), but when receiving a Radar Information Service must inform the ATSU what you intend to do.

G-CD, ROGER.

G-CD, DEVIZES.

G-CD, ROGER, PORTLAND REGIONAL PRESSURE SETTING 1004.

PORTLAND REGIONAL PRESSURE SETTING 1004, CAN YOU ADVISE THE STATUS OF DANGER AREA 123, G-CD.

G-CD, D123 BELIEVED TO BE ACTIVE, FREECALL SALISBURY OPERATIONS FOR DANGER AREA CROSSING SERVICE ON 122.750, RADAR SERVICE TERMINATED, SQUAWK SEVEN THOUSAND.

RADAR SERVICE TERMINATED, SQUAWK SEVEN THOUSAND, FREECALL SALISBURY OPERATIONS 122.750, G-CD.

Use of the instruction 'freecall' implies that the next frequency does not have your flight details, so a full message passing them will be required.

SALISBURY OPERATIONS, G-ABCD, REQUEST DANGER AREA CROSSING SERVICE FOR DANGER AREA 123.

G-ABCD, PASS YOUR DETAILS.

Note that the ATC unit has continued to use the full callsign so you must continue to do so as well.

G-ABCD IS A CESSNA 172, FROM KEMBLE TO BRISTOL VIA HENSTRIDGE, 1 MILE SOUTH WEST DEVIZES, THREE THOUSAND FEET PORTLAND PRESSURE SETTING 1004, VMC, ESTIMATE HENSTRIDGE AT 35.

G-ABCD, FLIGHT INFORMATION SERVICE, CROSSING APPROVED.

FLIGHT INFORMATION SERVICE, CROSSING APPROVED, G-ABCD.

G-ABCD, REPORT VACATING THE DANGER AREA.

WILCO, G-ABCD.

Southeast of Warminster:

LEAVING DANGER AREA 123, G-ABCD.

G-ABCD, ROGER, FLIGHT INFORMATION SERVICE TERMINATED.

G-ABCD, FLIGHT INFORMATION SERVICE TERMINATED, CHANGING TO YEOVILTON 127.350.

G-ABCD, ROGER.

YEOVILTON APPROACH, G-ABCD, REQUEST LARS.

Although now in uncontrolled airspace where there is no requirement to talk to any ATSU, good airmanship dictates that if a service is available it is a good idea to use it.

G-ABCD, PASS YOUR MESSAGE.

G-ABCD IS A CESSNA 172, FROM KEMBLE TO BRISTOL VIA HENSTRIDGE, 2 MILES SOUTH EAST WARMINSTER, THREE THOUSAND FEET PORTLAND PRESSURE SETTING 1004, VMC, ESTIMATE HENSTRIDGE AT 35, REQUEST RADAR INFORMATION SERVICE.

Although a Radar Service was requested on first contact, no service is in operation until specifically stated by the controller.

G-CD, SQUAWK 0214.

SQUAWK 0214, G-CD.

G-CD, IDENTIFIED 2 MILES SOUTH EAST WARMINSTER, RADAR INFORMATION SERVICE, REPORT HENSTRIDGE.

RADAR INFORMATION SERVICE, WILCO, G-CD.

YEOVILTON, G-CD, OVERHEAD HENSTRIDGE, TURNING ON TRACK CHEDDAR, REQUEST MATZ PENETRATION.

G-CD, CLEARED TO CROSS THE YEOVILTON MATZ ON TRACK TO CHEDDAR AT THREE THOUSAND FEET ON YEOVILTON QFE 1001, REPORT ABEAM WELLS.

CLEARED TO CROSS THE MATZ ON TRACK TO CHEDDAR AT THREE THOUSAND FEET, YEOVILTON QFE 1001, WILCO, G-CD.

ABEAM WELLS, G-CD.

G-CD, SQUAWK 4618.

SQUAWK 4618, G-CD.

G-CD, RADAR SERVICE TERMINATED, CONTACT BRISTOL APPROACH 125.650.

RADAR SERVICE TERMINATED, CONTACT BRISTOL APPROACH 125.650, G-CD.

The controller has used the word 'CONTACT', implying that flight details have been passed to Bristol, so an abbreviated message can be used for the first call.

BRISTOL APPROACH, G-ABCD, APPROACHING CHEDDAR, DESCENDING TO TWO THOUSAND FEET, SQUAWK 4618, REQUEST JOINING INSTRUCTIONS.

G-CD, BRISTOL APPROACH, STANDBY.

No response is required to 'standby' (i.e. no need for the reply 'STANDBY, G-CD'), as the controller should get back to you in due course. No onward clearance is implied, so do not enter controlled airspace.

If, however, following a suitable period you don't hear back, and there's no obvious reason why, it may be appropriate to remind the controller you are still waiting:

BRISTOL APPROACH, G-CD, HOLDING AT CHEDDAR.

G-CD, WHEN INSTRUCTED EXPECT A STANDARD CHEDDAR VFR ARRIVAL RUNWAY 27, NOT ABOVE TWO THOUSAND FEET ON THE BRISTOL QNH 1005.

WHEN INSTRUCTED EXPECT A STANDARD CHEDDAR VFR ARRIVAL RUNWAY 27, NOT ABOVE TWO THOUSAND FEET ON THE BRISTOL QNH 1005, G-CD.

Again, no onward clearance is implied so do not enter controlled airspace.

G-CD, CORRECT, FOR ONWARD CLEARANCE CONTACT BRISTOL TOWER 133.850.

CONTACT BRISTOL TOWER 133.850, G-CD.

BRISTOL TOWER, G-ABCD, CHEDDAR, REQUEST JOINING INSTRUCTIONS.

G-CD, CLEARED TO ENTER CONTROLLED AIRSPACE, JOIN DOWNWIND LEFT HAND RUNWAY 27, BRISTOL QFE 983 MILLIBARS.

CLEARED TO ENTER CONTROLLED AIRSPACE TO JOIN DOWNWIND LEFT HAND 27, BRISTOL QFE 983 MILLIBARS, G-CD.

G-CD, CORRECT, REPORT APPROACHING CHURCHILL.

WILCO, G-CD.

In the exchange above, the instruction was to 'JOIN DOWNWIND', so this represents the clearance limit – the furthest position to which the aircraft can proceed without further clearance.

The subsequent instruction to 'REPORT APPROACHING CHURCHILL' (a point before downwind) is therefore merely a request for a position report and so can be answered with 'WILCO'.

APPROACHING CHURCHILL, G-CD.

G-CD, YOU'RE NUMBER TWO TO A SENECA CROSSWIND, ARE YOU VISUAL WITH THE TRAFFIC.

AFFIRM, G-CD.

G-CD, CONTINUE INBOUND, REPORT DOWNWIND.

WILCO, G-CD.

Again, 'CONTINUE INBOUND, REPORT DOWNWIND', is merely confirmation of an already issued clearance, so 'WILCO' is fine in reply. Had the controller wished to change his mind and hold you at Churchill this would have represented an amendment to the clearance, and so would have to have been read back in full.

G-CD, DOWNWIND.

G-CD, NUMBER 2 TO THE SENECA, REPORT FINAL 27.

NUMBER 2 TO THE SENECA, REPORT FINAL 27, G-CD.

Since the previous clearance limit was left base, the instruction 'REPORT FINAL TWO SEVEN' is effectively an onward clearance, and so should be read back in full.

If a clearance limit is reached/approached without further instructions, contact the controller or, if this is not possible, hold (orbit) at the clearance limit.

The above series of exchanges serve to illustrate the importance of maintaining an awareness of your clearance limit.

FINAL 27, G-CD.

G-CD, RUNWAY 27, LAND AFTER THE SENECA, SURFACE WIND 250 7 KNOTS.

RUNWAY 27, LAND AFTER THE SENECA, G-CD

G-CD, GO AROUND, I SAY AGAIN, GO AROUND, ACKNOWLEDGE.

GOING AROUND, G-CD.

G-CD, LEFT HAND CIRCUIT, REPORT DOWNWIND.

LEFT HAND CIRCUIT, REPORT DOWNWIND, G-CD.

G-CD, DOWNWIND.

G-CD, REPORT BEFORE LEFT BASE.

REPORT BEFORE LEFT BASE, G-CD.

READY FOR LEFT BASE, G-CD.

G-CD, TRAFFIC IS A BRITISH AIRWAYS EMBRAER JET ON A 6 MILE FINAL, DO YOU HAVE THE TRAFFIC IN SIGHT.

NEGATIVE, G-CD.

G-CD, ORBIT RIGHT PRESENT POSITION, REPORT WHEN YOU HAVE THE TRAFFIC IN SIGHT.

ORBIT RIGHT PRESENT POSITION, WILCO, G-CD.

VISUAL WITH THE EMBRAER, G-CD.

G-CD, RUNWAY 27, NUMBER 2 TO THAT TRAFFIC, REPORT FINAL, CAUTION VORTEX WAKE, RECOMMENDED SPACING 4 MILES.

NUMBER TWO TO THE TRAFFIC, REPORT FINAL 27, REQUEST 1 FURTHER ORBIT FOR SPACING, G-CD.

G-CD, APPROVED, REPORT ROLLING OUT ON BASE.

WILCO, G-CD.

G-CD, ROLLING OUT ON BASE.

G-CD, ROGER, RUNWAY 27 REPORT FINAL.

REPORT FINAL 27, G-CD.

FINAL 27, G-CD.

G-CD, WIND 250 7 KNOTS, CLEARED TO LAND RUNWAY 27.

CLEAR TO LAND RUNWAY 27, G-CD.

WIND 220 9 KNOTS,

No reply is required to additional wind reports.

G-CD, KEEP YOUR SPEED UP, VACATE AT FOXTROT, JET TRAFFIC ON 3 MILE FINAL, EXPEDITE.

EXPEDITE VACATING AT FOXTROT, G-CD.

Once clear of the holding point:

G-CD, VACATED.

G-CD, ROGER, CONTACT GROUND 121.925.

CONTACT GROUND 121.925, G-CD.

BRISTOL GROUND, G-ABCD, VACATED AT FOXTROT.

G-CD, BRISTOL GROUND, TAXI TO THE CLUB APRON AND REPORT SHUTTING DOWN.

TAXI TO THE CLUB APRON, WILCO, G-CD.

Club apron:

G-CD, SHUTTING DOWN.

G-CD, ROGER.

While the flight above is generally similar to the type of scenarios used in the test, remember that at some point there will be an emergency involving either the candidate or another aircraft.

CHAPTER 9 INSTRUMENT PROCEDURES AND PHRASEOLOGY

This chapter is intended to be of use to private pilots adding an instrument qualification to their licence, and those pilots going on to professional licences and commercial operations. The content is largely outside the syllabus of the FRTOL test.

ENGINE START AND TAXI

Commercial aircraft parked nose into a stand may need to be pushed back from the stand by a tug, and for jet aircraft this is usually done concurrently with engine start:

BRISTOL TOWER, BRITISH 12 ALPHA, EMBRAER 145, ON STAND 16, REQUEST PUSH AND START, INFORMATION UNIFORM, QNH 1005.

BRITISH 12 ALPHA, PUSH AND START APPROVED TO FACE SOUTH.

PUSH AND START APPROVED TO FACE SOUTH, BRITISH 12 ALPHA.

Turboprop aircraft usually start on the stand, but may be able to reverse off the stand under their own power using reverse thrust. This is referred to as 'POWER BACK':

GLASGOW GROUND, BRITISH 23 BRAVO, REQUEST POWER BACK STAND 9.

Larger airfields will have Low Visibility Procedures (LVPs) that are instituted when conditions fall below certain predetermined minima. With LVPs in force the number of runway entry points in use may be restricted, and some taxiways closed. Additionally, runway holding points further back from the runway than those used in good conditions may be used to protect the ILS signal.

Some airfields are equipped with red stop bars – a line of red lights – across their taxiways which are used in low-visibility conditions. If a red stop bar is approached when a clearance to taxi to a point beyond the stop bar has already been received, this should be queried with the controller:

GROUND, BRITISH 12 ALPHA, CLEARED ALPHA 2, APPROACHING A RED STOP BAR AT ZULU 3.

Usually this will merely be an oversight, and the bar will be extinguished. If, however, for some technical reason this is not possible, an illuminated red stop bar must only be crossed with the express permission of ATC.

DEPARTURE CLEARANCES

Flights departing non-airways are cleared to depart controlled airspace with a routing and level:

WESSEX 10, CLEARED TO LEAVE THE ZONE IFR, ON TRACK BRECON, CLIMB AND MAINTAIN FIVE THOUSAND FEET.

When a flight plan is constructed it is not possible to know which runway will be in use at the time of departure. To cope with this the flight plan will include the point of departure (airfield) and the first point on the airway system (the airways joining point), but not how to get from one to the other. This routing is then passed by ATC just prior to departure. At very large airfields there may be a dedicated 'Clearance Delivery' frequency who should be contacted before engine start. Where there isn't a 'Clearance Delivery' frequency the clearance will be passed by 'Ground' or 'Tower', and this may be done during the taxi.

For flights departing into the airways system the type of route clearance received will depend on whether or not the airfield is directly connected to the airways system by controlled airspace.

Where the airport is not connected to the airways system, the clearance will be somewhat long-winded as it has include details such as the initial airway, joining point, level and cruise level:

BRITISH 12 ALPHA, I HAVE YOUR CLEARANCE.

GO AHEAD, BRITISH 12 ALPHA.

BRITISH 12 ALPHA, CLEARED TO PARIS CHARLES DE GAUL VIA LIMA 9, JOIN CONTROLLED AIRSPACE AT WOTAN, LEVEL FLIGHT LEVEL 90, REQUEST LEVEL CHANGE ON ROUTE FLIGHT LEVEL 230, SQUAWK 5135.

Because the airfield is not joined to the airways system there will be a period of flight in uncontrolled airspace, but the clearance to the airways joining point implies that permission to re-enter controlled airspace is already given. The instruction 'LEVEL, FLIGHT LEVEL 90' means that the aircraft must have reached flight level 90 by the airway boundary, if the clearance had allowed the aircraft to enter controlled airspace while still climbing it would have read 'CLIMBING FLIGHT LEVEL 90'.

Those airports that are directly connected to the airways system will use Standard Instrument Departures (SIDs). There will be one or more SID from each runway to each of the airways joining points used by that airport. SIDs are named for the point they lead to, so for example at Birmingham the SID leading from runway 33 to the Cowly airways joining point is designated the COWLY 2 DELTA, while from runway 15 it is the COWLY 1 ECHO. Since the SID details route, maximum and minimum levels to be achieved at points along the SID, and speeds, the departure clearance will be relatively short:

BRITISH 12 ALPHA, CLEARED TO FRANKFURT VIA THE COWLY 2 DELTA, SQUAWK 6315.

All these are clearances and so must be read back, and may be subsequently amended by a local departure clearance:

BRITISH 12 ALPHA, AFTER DEPARTURE CLIMB STRAIGHT AHEAD UNTIL INSTRUCTED BY RADAR.

On transfer to Approach/Departure the pilot should provide the following information:

1. callsign;
2. level, or passing level and cleared level if climbing; and
3. SID designator or routing or heading, as appropriate:

LONDON, BRITISH 12 ALPHA, FLIGHT LEVEL 43, CLIMBING 70, COWLY 2 DELTA DEPARTURE.

EN ROUTE

When operating in IMC outside controlled airspace, there is no requirement to talk to ATC; however, most pilots will want to receive a radar service such as a RIS or RAS where this is available. The phraseology used when operating in IMC outside controlled airspace is generally the same as for VMC operation, and has been discussed along with radar service phraseology in Chapter 5.

Airways flying is, from the R/T point of view, in some respects relatively easy. Each controller will tell you when to contact the next controller without you having to worry about airspace boundaries, and since the change from one frequency to another is by 'handover' the new controller will already have the flight details. The initial contact message can therefore be quite short:

1. callsign;
2. level, or passing level and cleared level if climbing or descending; and
3. routing or heading:

SWISS CONTROL, BRITISH 12 ALPHA, FLIGHT LEVEL 370, TOWARDS MOBLO.

RHINE RADAR, BRITISH 12 ALPHA, PASSING FLIGHT LEVEL THREE HUNDRED, DESCENDING FLIGHT LEVEL 250, HEADING 155.

REPORTING POINTS

Reporting points and airways were originally defined by reference to ground-based navaids, usually VHF Omni Range (VOR) beacons. All these beacons have a name based on their geographical location, and have a corresponding three-letter identification code. When directing an aircraft to route to one of these points, the controller can use either the name:

WESSEX 10, ROUTE DIRECT BRECON.

... or the three-letter identification code (which in the case of Brecon is BCN):

WESSEX 10, ROUTE DIRECT BRAVO CHARLIE NOVEMBER.

This three-letter identification code is how the point will appear in flight plans and GPS/Flight Management System (FMS) databases.

With the advent of DME it became easy to define other points as a bearing and distance from a beacon, and with the arrival of GPS and Flight Management Systems, it has become possible to designate waypoints at any arbitrary point in space, with or without reference to a beacon. All these waypoints that are not located overhead a navaid are given a five-letter name, which may reflect their location: REXAM is near the town of Wrexham and NEDUL is overhead The Needles on the Isle of Weight. Others may be more fanciful: the next point out from NEDUL, which is over the sea and so not near anything much, is called THRED.

When directing an aircraft to route to one of these waypoints, the controller will use the name, which is also how the point will appear in flight plans and GPS/FMS databases. In order to input these points into a GPS/FMS they must be spelt correctly, so if a controller names a beacon that you don't know the three-letter code for, or if the spelling of the name of a waypoint is not obvious from its name, ask the controller to spell it out:

BRITISH 12 ALPHA, ROUTE DIRECT HAREM THEN DINKELSBUHL.

DIRECT HAREM THEN DINKELSBUHL, REQUEST YOU SPELL THOSE POINTS, BRITISH 12 ALPHA.

BRITISH 12 ALPHA, HAREM, HOTEL ALPHA ROMEO ECHO MIKE, DINKELSBUHL, DELTA KILO BRAVO.

HOTEL ALPHA ROMEO ECHO MIKE, AND DELTA KILO BRAVO, BRITISH 12 ALPHA.

LEVEL INSTRUCTIONS

Normally no particular rate of climb or descent is specified, but in controlled airspace it is generally expected that a rate of not less than 500ft/min will be maintained, though there is some national variation in this – in French airspace it is 1,000ft/min. If it is not possible to maintain the required rate, for whatever reason, the controller should be informed.

Occasionally a rapid climb or descent will be required, in which case the controller will use the word 'EXPEDITE':

BRITISH 12 ALPHA, EXPEDITE CLIMB FLIGHT LEVEL 250.

Or sometimes a specific rate is required:

BRITISH 12 ALPHA, DESCEND FLIGHT LEVEL 120, RATE ONE THOUSAND FIVE HUNDRED FEET PER MINUTE OR MORE.

While it is usually expected that the climb or descent will be started as soon as the instruction is issued, in some circumstances the controller may leave the decision when to begin the manoeuvre up to the pilot by using the phrase 'WHEN READY'. This kind of instruction is often issued in conjunction with a specific point or time at which the manoeuvre has to be completed. It is then up to the pilot to plan his climb or descent to reach the specified level by the specified point or time:

BRITISH 12 ALPHA, WHEN READY DESCEND FLIGHT LEVEL 120, TO BE LEVEL 10 MILES BEFORE COMPTON.

WHEN READY DESCEND FLIGHT LEVEL 120, TO BE LEVEL 10 MILES BEFORE COMPTON, BRITISH 12 ALPHA.

The pilot should then inform the controller when he has left the original level and started the climb or descent:

BRITISH 12 ALPHA, LEAVING FLIGHT LEVEL TWO HUNDRED, DESCENDING FLIGHT LEVEL 120.

ARRIVAL

Initial contact with the ATSU at the arrival airfield will usually be on the 'Approach' frequency, or 'Tower' if an approach frequency is not available.

Flights operating outside controlled airspace may have to 'freecall' the appropriate controller with full details, using the 'initial call' format discussed in earlier chapters, though if a radar service is already being received there may be co-ordination between that ATSU and the airfield ATSU, and a handover might be arranged. In any event the initial exchange should include the designation letter of the ATIS if this has been received.

BRISTOL APPROACH, G-ABCD.

G-CD, BRISTOL APPROACH, PASS YOUR MESSAGE.

G-CD, CESSNA 172, FROM COVENTRY TO BRISTOL, 15 MILES SOUTH EAST BRECON, FIVE THOUSAND FIVE HUNDRED FEET COTSWOLD QNH 1010, IFR, ESTIMATE ZONE BOUNDARY AT 35, SQUAWKING 1523, WITH INFORMATION GOLF.

Irrespective of any radar service being received, or flight plan filed, you must not enter controlled airspace until a clearance to do so has been issued.

Once in communication with the ATSU the controller will pass heading or routing and level instructions. A little common sense is required here, because the phrase 'CLEARED TO ENTER CONTROLLED AIRSPACE' may not be used during subsequent radio exchanges, so if the controlling ATSU issues a specific instruction that will take the aircraft into controlled airspace this can be taken as constituting clearance to enter:

G-CD, IDENTIFIED, ROUTE DIRECT TO THE BRAVO ROMEO INDIA, DESCEND TO ALTITUDE FOUR THOUSAND FEET, BRISTOL QNH 1008.

DIRECT TO THE BRAVO ROMEO INDIA, DESCEND TO ALTITUDE FOUR THOUSAND FEET, BRISTOL QNH 1008, G-CD.

G-CD, CORRECT, INFORMATION GOLF CURRENT, EXPECT RADAR VECTORS TO THE ILS, RUNWAY 27.

EXPECT RADAR VECTORS TO THE ILS, RUNWAY 27, G-CD.

Here the controller has specified the type of approach in use. If, say for training purposes, a different type of approach or some holds were required, this would be a good time to make that request.

For flights operating in the airways system the type of arrival will again depend on whether or not the airfield is directly connected to the airways system by controlled airspace. When approaching an airfield not joined to the airways system there will be a period of flight in uncontrolled airspace, and the same considerations described above will apply; in practice, however, the ATC service will tend to be seamless as transfer to the airfield ATSU will be by handover.

Where the airfield is directly connected to the airways system arriving aircraft will route via a Standard Arrival, known as a Star. A Star is basically the opposite of a SID, and like a SID details the route, levels and speeds to be achieved at points along the route. A Star routes the aircraft in as far as the waypoint that is the clearance limit for that arrival, the idea being that sometime before the clearance limit is reached the aircraft is re-cleared onwards by being given further route instructions, radar vectors or clearance for a procedural approach. As with a SID, the arrival takes its name from the point it leads to:

BRITISH 12 ALPHA, CLEARED THE LANAK 1 ALPHA ARRIVAL.

CLEARED THE LANAK 1 ALPHA ARRIVAL, BRITISH 12 ALPHA.

In the event of the clearance limit being reached without onward clearance being received (or in the event of radio failure) the approach plate will detail what to do, which will usually involve entering a holding pattern. However, if there is no obvious reason why you haven't been given further clearance, it may be possible to remind the controller of your presence:

GLASGOW APPROACH, BRITISH 12 ALPHA, APPROACHING LANAK.

BRITISH 12 ALPHA, ROGER, LEAVE LANAK HEADING 015.

LEAVE LANAK HEADING 015, BRITISH 12 ALPHA.

At busier airfields part of the approach may be handled by a radar approach controller with the callsign 'DIRECTOR'. When instructed to 'CONTACT

DIRECTOR' the initial message should consist of callsigns only – nothing else – unless otherwise instructed by 'Approach':

GLASGOW DIRECTOR, BRITISH 12 ALPHA.

HOLDING

When a controller needs to delay a flight's onward progress he may direct it to route to a holding fix, usually a beacon, to take up the hold:

WESSEX 10, ROUTE DIRECT TO THE BRAVO ROMEO INDIA TO TAKE UP THE HOLD.

DIRECT TO THE BRAVO ROMEO INDIA, TAKE UP THE HOLD, WESSEX 10.

An idea of how long the delay is likely to be may be gained if the controller passes an 'Expected Arrival Time' (EAT), the time at which he expects to be able to allow the aircraft to commence its approach:

WESSEX 10, EXPECTED ARRIVAL TIME 15.

E.A.T. 15, WESSEX 10.

The method of entry to the holding pattern depends on the aircraft's heading inbound to the holding fix: it may be possible to enter the hold directly, or a joining procedure (such as a parallel or teardrop join) may have to be performed. The pilot should make a report when overhead the holding fix, though the phraseology of this report is affected by the type of entry:

- If a direct entry is possible, the phrase 'TAKING UP THE HOLD' is used.
- If a joining procedure has to be performed, the phrase 'BEACON JOINING' is used the first time over the beacon when turning outbound for the joining procedure. Then, having completed the joining manoeuvre, report 'TAKING UP THE HOLD' next time over the beacon when turning into the holding pattern itself.

WESSEX 10, BEACON JOINING.

WESSEX 10, ROGER, REPORT TAKING UP THE HOLD.

WILCO, WESSEX 10.

WESSEX 10, TAKING UP THE HOLD.

WESSEX 10. ROGER.

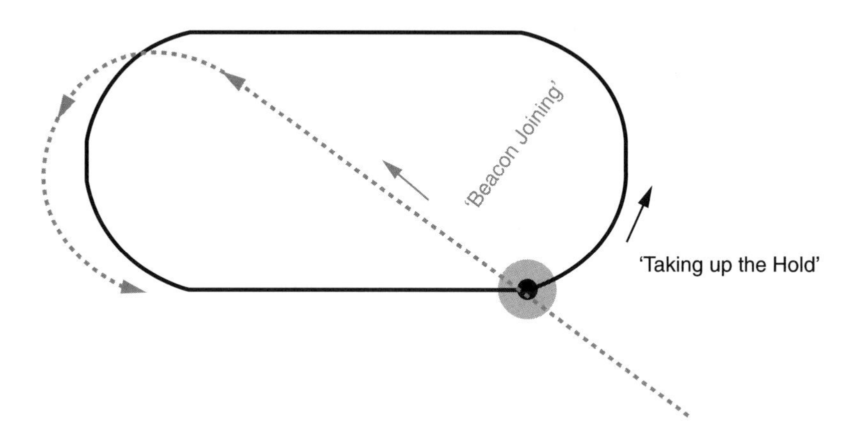

Calls is the holding pattern.

Once established in the holding pattern the hold should be continued until instructed otherwise. When the controller is ready for the aircraft to continue, onward clearance may be in the form of route instructions, radar vectors or clearance for a procedural approach:

WESSEX 10, HOLD CANCELLED, TURN LEFT, HEADING SOUTH.

ROGER TURN LEFT, HEADING SOUTH, WESSEX 10.

In the exchange above the turn would have been made from the position of the aircraft at the time of the instruction, alternatively the controller may wish the aircraft to continue in the hold until the holding fix is reached, and then continue the approach from that point:

WESSEX 10, NEXT TIME OVER THE BEACON, CLEARED OUTBOUND WITH THE PROCEDURE.

APPROACH

Whatever the type of initial arrival, the aircraft has to eventually end up on the final approach path. This is achieved by either Radar-Vectored Approach or a Procedural Approach.

Radar-Vectored Approach

The radar controller passes the pilot a series of heading and level instructions that manoeuvre the aircraft onto the final approach path.

BRITISH 12 ALPHA, RIGHT TURN HEADING 020 DEGREES.

RIGHT TURN HEADING 020 DEGREES, BRITISH 12 ALPHA.

BRITISH 12 ALPHA, DESCEND TO ALTITUDE SIX THOUSAND FEET, QNH 1001.

DESCEND TO ALTITUDE SIX THOUSAND FEET, QNH 1001, BRITISH 12 ALPHA.

BRITISH 12 ALPHA, YOU HAVE APPROXIMATELY 25 TRACK MILES, WILL THAT BE SUFFICIENT TO LOSE THE ALTITUDE.

AFFIRM, BRITISH 12 ALPHA.

Track mileages to touchdown are passed to aid descent planning, or if the controller is concerned that there may not be enough distance to allow the altitude to be lost. If the pilot was concerned that he might not have enough distance to lose the height, he could have asked to be given more track mileage by using the phrase 'REQUEST FURTHER VECTORS'.

BRITISH 12 ALPHA, REDUCE SPEED TWO HUNDRED KNOTS OR LESS, NUMBER 3 IN TRAFFIC, NUMBER 2 IS TWELVE MILES AHEAD, SHORTS 360.

SPEED TWO HUNDRED KNOTS OR LESS, ROGER, BRITISH 12 ALPHA.

Speed instructions are given to allow the controller to allow sequencing, and to maintain separation between traffic.

BRITISH 12 ALPHA, DESCEND TO ALTITUDE THREE THOUSAND FIVE HUNDRED FEET.

DESCEND TO ALTITUDE THREE THOUSAND FIVE HUNDRED FEET, BRITISH 12 ALPHA.

BRITISH 12 ALPHA, TURN LEFT HEADING 300 DEGREES, BASE LEG.

TURN LEFT HEADING 300 DEGREES, BASE LEG, BRITISH 12 ALPHA.

BRITISH 12 ALPHA, TURN LEFT HEADING 265, CLOSING FROM THE LEFT, REPORT LOCALISER ESTABLISHED.

TURN LEFT HEADING 265, CLOSE FROM THE LEFT, REPORT LOCALISER ESTABLISHED, BRITISH 12 ALPHA.

Here the clearance is to establish on the localiser only, i.e. not descend with the glideslope. Had the controller used 'ILS' instead of 'localiser' this would have implied clearance to establish on the glideslope as well.

LOCALISER ESTABLISHED, BRITISH 12 ALPHA.

BRITISH 12 ALPHA, DESCEND ON THE ILS, CONTACT TOWER 118.8.

DESCEND ON THE ILS, CONTACT TOWER 118.8, BRITISH 12 ALPHA.

TOWER, BRITISH 12 ALPHA, LOCALISER ESTABLISHED RUNWAY 23, 10 MILES.

Had the glideslope already been intercepted the pilot would use the phrase 'FULLY ESTABLISHED' instead of 'LOCALISER ESTABLISHED'.

On first contact with the tower the runway designation should be stated as a final check. This is particularly important at airports with parallel runways, but a good habit to get into anywhere.

BRITISH 12 ALPHA, CONTINUE APPROACH.

CONTINUE APPROACH RUNWAY 23, BRITISH 12 ALPHA.

BRITISH 12 ALPHA, RUNWAY 23 CLEARED TO LAND.

CLEARED TO LAND RUNWAY 23, BRITISH 12 ALPHA.

The word ESTABLISHED has a specific meaning in relation to the inbound track of an approach. For an ILS or localiser approach the aircraft is considered to be 'LOCALISER ESTABLISHED' when the ILS needle indicates half-scale deflection or less.

Where an approach other than an ILS is being flown, the controller will ask the pilot to report 'ESTABLISHED ON THE INBOUND TRACK'. The criteria for considering the aircraft to be 'established' on the inbound track in these cases are:

VOR approach: Course Deviation Indicator half-scale deflection or less.

NDB approach: ADF needle indicating within 5 degrees of track.

Procedural Approach

The aircraft follows a fixed route defined by one or more waypoints (usually beacons), which allow it to be manoeuvred onto the final approach path usually via a base or procedure turn. The approach plate will specify the levels to be achieved at points along the approach:

APPROACH, WESSEX 10, REQUEST NDB DME APPROACH.

WESSEX 10, ROGER, EXPECT AN NDB DME APPROACH, RUNWAY 27.

EXPECT AN NDB DME APPROACH, RUNWAY 27, WESSEX 10.

WESSEX 10, CORRECT, NEXT TIME OVER THE BEACON, CLEARED OUTBOUND WITH THE PROCEDURE, QFE 987 MILLIBARS, REPORT BEACON OUTBOUND.

NEXT TIME OVER THE BEACON, CLEARED OUTBOUND WITH THE PROCEDURE, QFE 987 MILLIBARS, WILCO, WESSEX 10.

The 'BEACON OUTBOUND' call is made at the final passage over the beacon when turning outbound with the procedure.

Clearance 'WITH THE PROCEDURE' implies that both the track and descent profile detailed on the approach plate are to be followed.

BEACON OUTBOUND, WESSEX 10.

WESSEX 10, ROGER, REPORT BASE TURN [or PROCEDURE TURN] COMPLETE.

WILCO, WESSEX 10.

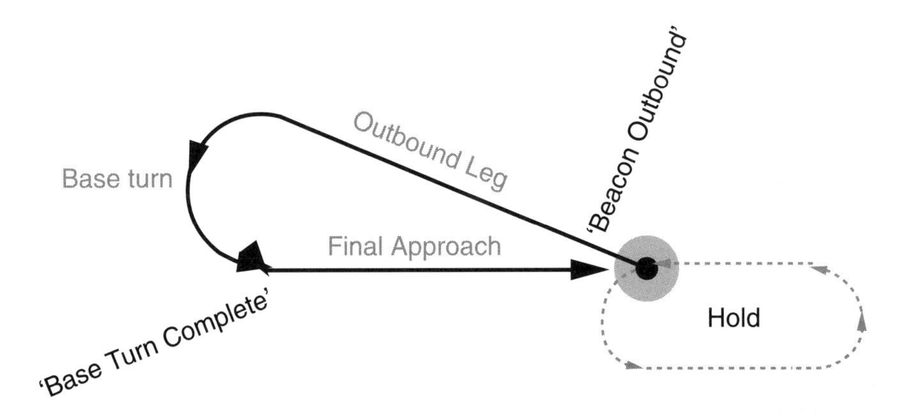

Calls during a procedural approach.

The 'BASE TURN COMPLETE' call is made when the base turn is completed and the aircraft is established on the inbound track. If the procedure uses a procedure turn instead of a base turn, the phrase 'PROCEDURE TURN COMPLETE' is used instead.

✈ BASE TURN [*or* PROCEDURE TURN] COMPLETE, WESSEX 10.

AFTER LANDING

When LVPs are in force the number of runway turn-off points available may be restricted. The controller may request a pilot to inform him when he has vacated the runway. A 'sterile area' indicated by alternating amber and green taxiway centreline lighs may be needed to protect the ILS signal. When LVPs are in force the 'RUNWAY VACATED' call should not be made until clear of this area.

APPENDIX I
SSR TRANSPONDER OPERATION AND PHRASEOLOGY

A transponder (transmitter & responder) is a device that sends a reply back to Air Traffic Control in response to an interrogation signal generated by a Secondary Surveillance Radar (SSR). The reply is encoded with data selected by the pilot, but once this has been set up, no further input is required unless the settings need to be changed. The data received by Air Traffic is displayed to the controller as a data block superimposed on the aircraft's primary return on the plan position indicator (radar screen).

MODES OF OPERATION

Mode A identifies the primary radar return by a four-figure code: this is the 'squawk' selected by the pilot. This code will either be that instructed by the ATSU, or one of the special-purpose codes (*see* below). Once received, the code can be displayed to the controller 'raw' or manipulated by the ATSU computers to show information such as flight number or destination.

Mode C provides the information described above but also, via an input from the aircraft altimeter, provides a readout of the aircraft's level based on pressure setting 1013Mb; however, this may be manipulated at the ATSU to show altitude instead of flight level.

Mode S is capable of handling large quantities of two-way data. This data linking is increasingly used in commercial operations to free up R/T bandwidth though (as yet) is not much used in General Aviation.

BASIC CONTROLS AND OPERATION

Function/mode selector: selects the operating status of the transponder. Usually a simple rotary knob with the positions listed below, but more sophisticated sets may present the information electronically and have settings for use with Traffic Collision Avoidance Systems (TCAS). The usual positions are:

OFF	
STANDBY	Powers up the transponder circuitry, but does not transmit a reply. Should be selected when changing the four-figure code, to prevent triggering alarms at ATC by inadvertent selection of one of the special-purpose codes. Newer sets may automatically enter standby during code change.
ON (ATC ON)	Mode A operation.
ALT (ATC ALT)	Mode A and C operation.
TEST	Activates the test function, and typically illuminates the interrogation signal indicator.

Interrogation signal indicator: indicates when an interrogation signal is received.

Ident button: activates the 'special position identification' function, which causes the data block displayed on the controller's screen to be highlighted.

Code selector: selects the four-figure code that is to be transmitted to ATC. Each digit is between 0 and 7 (i.e. no 8s or 9s). Older sets usually have a separate knob for each digit; more modern sets display the data electronically via a single rotary selector.

TRANSPONDER CODES

Usually a pilot will select an individual code as instructed by ATC. For IFR/airways flight these are allocated centrally, while for VFR/local flights the code will indicate the controlling ATSU. For example, Bristol has codes 4610 to 4637 allocated for its use, so the first flight of the day requiring a code will be allocated 4610, the second 4611, and so on.

Otherwise, 'conspicuity' or a special-purpose codes may be selected as the situation warrants:

7000	CONSPICUITY. For use by any traffic in the UK FIR when a specific code has not been allocated by ATC.
7700	MAYDAY.
7600	RADIO FAILURE.
7500	HIJACK (unlawful interference in the conduct of the flight).

If you are having a problem remembering which code is which, try this rhyme:

Seven seven – going to heaven (Mayday)
Seven six – radio fix (Radio failure)
Seven five – taken alive (Hijack)

A special-purpose code will activate warning signals at the receiving ATSUs to draw the controllers' attention to a problem. To prevent accidental momentary activation during code change, older sets should be selected to 'standby' while changing the code. Newer sets may automatically revert to standby during code change – obviously, it is up to you to know your equipment.

OPERATION

While not all aircraft are fitted with transponders, VFR flights operating in controlled airspace or receiving an 'Air Traffic Service Outside Controlled Airspace' should squawk any code assigned if so equipped. Mode C should be selected unless otherwise specified. In the open FIR, if no code is allocated it is good airmanship to squawk 7000 for conspicuity.

'Standby' should usually selected when entering an airfield's traffic pattern to prevent clutter on the controller's display and to avoid nuisance warnings to TCAS-equipped aircraft. Local procedures may apply, though, so if in doubt you should check with the controller.

Generally speaking, IFR flights operating in controlled airspace will squawk the assigned code from take-off to landing, and at larger commercial airfields during taxiing as well.

☠ Assignment of a code does not, of itself, imply the provision of any particular Air Traffic or Radar Service.

PHRASEOLOGY SPECIFIC TO TRANSPONDER OPERATION

Transponder settings are 'required read back' items.

SQUAWK   Select code specified and set the mode.

G-CD, SQUAWK 5417.

SQUAWK 5417, G-CD.

If not transponder equipped, inform the controller:

UNABLE COMPLY, NEGATIVE TRANSPONDER, G-CD.

SQUAWK IDENT — Activate the 'special position identification' function.

BRITISH 12 ALPHA, SQUAWK IDENT.

SQUAWK IDENT, BRITISH 12 ALPHA.

SQUAWK CHARLIE — Set the transponder to mode C.

G-CD, SQUAWK CHARLIE.

SQUAWK CHARLIE, G-CD.

VERIFY YOUR LEVEL — Report your level. Used to verify the mode C altitude readout – the controller will be expecting the reported level and readout level to be within 200ft of each other.

WESSEX 10, VERIFY YOUR LEVEL.

TWO THOUSAND FIVE HUNDRED FEET, 1005, WESSEX 10.

CONFIRM SQUAWK — Confirm the code selected and the mode set.

G-CD, CONFIRM SQUAWK.

5417, MODE C, G-CD.

RE-CYCLE SQUAWK — Re-cycle the four-figure code set. Even if the correct code appears to have been set, the indication should be deselected and re-selected in case the mechanism has stuck.

G-CD, RE-CYCLE SQUAWK 5417.

RE-CYCLING SQUAWK 5417, G-CD.

SQUAWK STANDBY — Select the transponder to standby. Often used when transferring control to another unit, or when a VFR flight is about to enter an airfield traffic pattern.

WESSEX 10, SQUAWK STANDBY.

SQUAWK STANDBY, WESSEX 10.

SQUAWK 7000	Select the conspicuity code. Often used when transferring control to another unit in the open FIR.

G-CD, HAWKSBURY RADAR, YOU'RE REACHING THE LIMIT OF MY RADAR COVERAGE, RADAR SERVICE TERMINATED, SQUAWK SEVEN THOUSAND, FREECALL HENFIELD INFORMATION 123.425.

RADAR SERVICE TERMINATED, SQUAWK SEVEN THOUSAND, FREECALL HENFIELD INFORMATION 123.425, G-CD.

Appendix II Radio Checks and Readability Scale

A radio-check transmission may be made at any time, but is usually made as a routine pre-flight check of radio serviceability, or when the pilot has cause to believe there may be a problem with the radio(s). A radio check transmission consists of the following:

1. callsign of the station being addressed;
2. callsign of the station making the transmission;
3. the phrase 'RADIO CHECK'; and
4. the frequency in use.

FRAMPTON GROUND, G-ABCD, RADIO CHECK, 121.7.

The reply will consist of:

1. callsign of the station making the check transmission;
2. callsign of the station replying; and
3. information on readability, which may employ the readability scale in the table below, and any other relevant information.

G-CD, FRAMPTON GROUND, READABILITY 5.

G-CD, FRAMPTON GROUND, READABILITY 3 WITH STATIC INTERFERENCE.

Readability Scale	Meaning
1	Unreadable
2	Readable now and then
3	Readable with difficulty
4	Readable
5	Perfectly readable

Appendix III Recorded Information Broadcasts

FORMAT OF ATIS AND VOLMET BROADCASTS

ATIS	Volmet
Message identification:	Aerodrome identification
1. Aerodrome identification	
2. ATIS letter (each message sequentially coded: A, B, C, etc.)	
3. Time of origination	
Runway in use (type of approach available)	
Surface wind	Surface wind
Visibility	Visibility
	Runway visual range
Weather (*see* table below)	Weather
Cloud (*see* table below)	Cloud
Temperature and dewpoint	Temperature and dewpoint
QNH (QFE)	QNH
Trend if applicable (*see* table below)	Trend if applicable
Essential aerodrome information:	
• Work in progress • Unserviceabilities • Runway surface state (*see* table below)	

STANDARD WORDS AND ABBREVIATIONS USED IN ATIS AND VOLMET BROADCASTS

Weather and Cloud

FEW	1 to 2 eighths (oktas) of sky covered by cloud
SCATTERED	3 to 4 eighths (oktas) of sky covered by cloud
BROKEN	5 to 7 eighths (oktas) of sky covered by cloud
OVERCAST	Sky completely covered by cloud (8 eighths)
CAVOK	No cloud below 5,000ft or sector safe altitude (whichever is greater), no cumulonimbus cloud, visibility greater than 10km, no significant weather.
SNOCLO	Airfield closed due to snow or snow clearance operations

Cloud type is not reported, unless this is significant, such as cumulonimbus or towering cumulus.

Runway Surface State:

DRY	Dry
DAMP	Surface shows a change of colour due to moisture
WET	Surface soaked with a film of moisture that is reflective
WATER PATCHES	Significant patches of standing water greater than 3mm deep covering 25% or more of the accessed area
FLOODED	Extensive patches of standing water greater than 3mm deep covering 50% or more of the accessed area

1. *For reporting purposes the runway is divided into three parts (touchdown zone, mid zone and stop end), and a report is passed for each third, e.g. 'WET, WET, DAMP'.*
2. *Braking action may be provided.*

SPECIMEN ATIS AND VOLMET BROADCASTS

These are transcripts of the ATIS and Volmet messages for Birmingham at 12.50 UTC on 26 July 2005.

ATIS, Birmingham

BIRMINGHAM INFORMATION DELTA, TIME 1250, RUNWAY IN USE 15, SURFACE WIND 080, 6 KNOTS, VARYING 030 TO 120 DEGREES, VISIBILITY TEN KILOMETRES OR MORE, CLOUD SCATTERED TWO THOUSAND FOUR HUNDRED FEET, BROKEN SIX THOUSAND FEET, TEMPERATURE 17, DEWPOINT 11, QNH 1011, ACKNOWLEDGE RECEIPT OF INFORMATION DELTA, REPORT AIRCRAFT TYPE ON FIRST CONTACT WITH AIR TRAFFIC CONTROL.

Volmet, London South

THIS IS LONDON VOLMET SOUTH; BIRMINGHAM, 1250, WIND 080, 6 KNOTS, VARYING BETWEEN 030 AND 120 DEGREES, VISIBILITY TEN KILOMETRES OR MORE, CLOUD SCATTERED TWO THOUSAND FOUR HUNDRED FEET, BROKEN SIX THOUSAND FEET, TEMPERATURE 17, DEWPOINT 11, QNH 1011; BOURNEMOUTH, 1250 etc...

Volmet Broadcasts in the British Isles

Volmet	Frequency	Airfields Covered
London Main	135.375	Amsterdam, Brussels, Dublin, Glasgow, Gatwick, Heathrow, Stansted, Manchester, Paris Charles de Gaulle
London South	128.600	Birmingham, Bournemouth, Bristol, Cardiff, Jersey, Luton, Norwich, Southampton, Southend
London North	126.600	Humberside, Nottingham East Midlands, Isle of Man, Leeds Bradford, Liverpool, Gatwick, Manchester, Newcastle, Durham Tees Valley
Scottish	125.725	Aberdeen, Belfast Aldergrove, Edinburgh, Glasgow, Inverness, Heathrow, Prestwick, Stornoway, Sumburgh
Dublin	127.000	Dublin, Shannon, Cork, Belfast Aldergrove, Glasgow, Prestwick, Manchester, Heathrow, Gatwick

APPENDIX IV MORSE CODE AND 'Q' CODES

MORSE CODE

Morse code, one of the earliest forms of radiotelephony, consists of transmitting each letter by a series of 'dots' (short tones) and 'dashes' (long tones). The main advantages are that the equipment required is relatively unsophisticated, and the power required is less than for voice transmission – put another way, you can get a greater range for a given power output. The disadvantages are that you have to know the code, and the message needs to be somewhat laboriously spelt out letter by letter. Today, the main remaining use of Morse in aviation is for navigation and approach aid identification, though even this is starting to be supplanted by voice identification.

A • • •
B – • • •
C – • – •
D – • •
E •
F • • – •
G – – •
H • • • •
I • •
J • – – –
K – • –
L • – • •
M – –
N – •
O – – –
P • – – •
Q – – • –
R • – •
S • • •
T –
U • • –
V • • • –
W • – –
X – • • –
Y – • – –
Z – – • •

'Q' CODES

A number of phrases occur repeatedly in day-to-day R/T, so to avoid having to spell them out each time (a laborious process when using Morse code) the 'Q' codes were developed. Each 'Q' code consists of a three-letter sequence beginning with Q and stands for a commonly used phrase, e.g. QSY means 'changing frequency to'. The use of a number of Q codes continued into voice R/T, and originally there were a considerable number of them;

however, the number in approved usage now is very small, and in fact the use of most, such as QSY, is actively discouraged. The few remaining that a pilot is likely come across are set out below:

QFE	Pressure setting which datum's the altimeter to the airfield height.
QNH	Pressure setting which datum's the altimeter to the mean sea level.
QNE	Altimeter reading at the threshold when 1013 is set on subscale.
QDM	Magnetic bearing to the station.
QDR	Magnetic bearing of the aircraft from the station.
QUJ	True bearing to the station.
QTE	True bearing of the aircraft from the station.
QGH	Approach based on headings to steer supplied by ATC.

Appendix V
FRTOL Syllabus

The CAA have produced the following syllabus of training for candidates for the FRTOL. The syllabus in the form of a checklist and other relevant information is available on the CAA website, www.caa.co.uk.

Familiarisation with Aircraft Equipment & Radio Licence

Aircraft Radio Equipment
Switching on
Selecting frequencies
Volume and squelch adjustment
Intercom and station box
Headset adjustment
Location of equipment
Location of antennae
Radio failure

Radio Licence and Procedures Aircraft Radio Licence and Schedule
FRTOL – ANO Schedule 8 and Article 21 Cap 413 – UK
AIP
Microphone technique
Callsigns and abbreviations
Listening out
Phonetic alphabet – standard phrases
Signal strength and readability reporting

Practical Training and Demonstration

Departure Procedures
Radio checks
Taxi information
Holding on the ground
Departure clearance
Take-off clearance
Frequency changing – ground/tower/approach
Difference between ATC/AFIS/AG
Conditional clearances
Use of SSR

En-Route Procedures
Frequency changing
Initial call
Procedural position reports
Level reporting
Use of FIS
Use of LARS
Use of SSR
MATZ penetration
SVFR clearances
Flight in a Control Zone
Obtaining VDF bearings for navigation

Circuit and Arrival Procedures
Initial call
Joining procedures (aerodrome information)
ATC clearance
Entering ATZ
Circuit call (incl. military circuits)
Landing orbit – extend – touch & go – go-around
Vacating runway
Closing down

Emergency and Lost Procedures
Mayday
Pan Pan – training fix
Obtaining VDF bearing
Degrees of emergency
Frequencies to use for emergencies
Priority of calls
Uncertainty of position
Radio failure
SSR emergency codes
Mayday relay – responsibilities
Cancelling emergency

INDEX